Catholic
Prayer
Book

For Louise and Harry France

CATHOLIC PRAYER BOOK

edited by *ANTHONY BULLEN*
priest of Liverpool Diocese

DARTON, LONGMAN & TODD

First published in Great Britain in 1970 by
Darton, Longman & Todd Ltd,
85 Gloucester Road, London SW7
© 1970 Anthony Bullen
The Jerusalem Bible © 1966 by Darton, Longman &
Todd, Ltd
and Doubleday & Company Inc.
New English translations of the Order of Mass, the
Rite of Baptism for Children and the
(provisional) Wedding Mass
including texts proper to England and Wales
(adapted to conform with the civil formula)
copyright © 1969 International Committee on English
in the Liturgy, Inc. All rights reserved.
The Order of Mass
Cum Originali Concordat, John Humphreys, J.C.D.,
9th January 1970.
Elsewhere in the book portions of texts, including
excerpts from provisional Rite of Ordination, and from
the Proper Prefaces, copyright © 1969, International
Committee on English in the Liturgy Inc, all rights
reserved.
Nihil Obstat: Thomas Worden, S.T.L., L.S.S., *Censor*
Imprimatur: ✠ George Andrew Beck, Archbishop of
Liverpool, 2nd February 1970
Printed in Great Britain by Cox & Wyman Ltd,
London, Reading and Fakenham
ISBN 0 232 51133 0

Contents

Acknowledgements

I am grateful to: Burns and Oates for permission to use two of Archbishop Goodier's prayers given in *The Life that is Light*, Gill and MacMillan Limited for Michel Quoist's prayer of sorrow from *Prayers of Life*, S.C.M. Press for an Easter prayer given by William Barclay in *Prayers for the Christian Year*, Geoffrey Chapman Ltd. for the 'Way of the Cross' from my book *Living and Believing*, Kevin Mayhew and Luke McNaughton for hymns from *Songs from the Psalms*, the Editors of *Catholic Education Today* for permission to reproduce a Service of Sorrow first published in that magazine, and to Father Gabriel, o.f.m., for permission to use the hymn published in *Masses Today*.

Quotations from Scripture are taken from the Jerusalem Bible. The use of 'thee' and 'thou', etc., is restricted to those prayers in which people are accustomed to this mode of address.

I should like to express my gratitude to Father Brian Newns for his advice, and to Miss Dorothy Head for editorial assistance.

Foreword

Those who love and practise their religion complain that in recent years they no longer find peace and rest when they go to Mass. Changes in the liturgy have been so frequent that they find it hard to follow what the priest is doing. Even the priest, they notice, has his problems. He no longer has one book but several and probably typewritten sheets as well to read. Most Catholics look back wistfully to the days when they could follow the Mass without effort in their missals. If they found the missal too difficult they could read their favourite prayers in the beloved *Garden of the Soul*.

Nothing therefore could be more opportune than this Catholic Prayer Book. Though intended for adults the text is simple and quite intelligible to older children. Those who use this prayer book may not be familiar with the modern catechetical approach upon which it is based. They will see that this new approach in no way discards the old devotions. Parents will find this book most helpful when they lead their children in family prayers each night. The short readings from scripture are admirably chosen.

I do not believe that young children have altered greatly in this generation in their attitude to religion. They turn easily and eagerly to our Lord. In their innocence they have an appetite for holy things. They will soon come to treasure this book and want one for their very own.

✠ JOHN CARD. HEENAN
Archbishop of Westminster.
Maundy Thursday 1970.

Part One

*FAMILY AND
PRIVATE PRAYERS*

Prayers for Every Day

We believe that when we were baptised God became a real Father to us, Jesus became our brother, the Holy Spirit began to live in us. We are personally known by name and loved by Father, Son and Spirit. Since this relationship of love exists, we will not want a day to go by without our speaking with Jesus to the Father, and listening to the Holy Spirit. Many christians try to speak to God and listen to him each morning and evening. In the morning we try to offer the day to him, our work, our joys, our sorrows and frustrations, our leisure. The christian feels 'in debt' to God. He gives thanks for the opportunity of using another day in the work of praising God, and of trying to make the world a better place, whether by typing, teaching, learning, cleaning, or any other job, so that at the end Christ may hand the world over to the Father.

Spontaneous made-up prayers on the lines of:

OFFERING – the day with Jesus to the Father
THANKING – the Father for another day
RESOLVING – to work for a better world

no matter how brief the prayers are, even if they be said while hurriedly dressing or on the way to school or work, may well be the best. For those who like to

have set prayers, or on those occasions when sponta-
neous praying is difficult, the following prayers may
be useful:

In the Morning

To the Father, King of ages who is immortal, invisible,
the one and only God, be honour and glory for ever and
ever, Amen.

Lord God, our Father all powerful, you have brought
us to the beginning of this day. By your power, keep us
on the road to salvation: do not let us fall into any sin
today but grant that all we say, all we think, all we do,
may tend towards your glory. We make this prayer to
you through Jesus Christ our Lord. Amen.

May holy Mary and all the saints plead for us with the
Lord that we may be helped and saved by him who lives
and reigns for ever. Amen.

In the Morning – (Alternative)

God my father believes in me.
Dear God my father you believe in me. You made me.
I believe in you and I believe that you are close to me. I
believe that wherever I go, you go. I believe that you
will be with me all through this day.

God my father trusts me.
Dear God my father, you trust me. You have given me
many gifts, family, friends, talents. I depend on you for
everything, and so I trust you completely. Without you
I can do nothing.

God my father loves me.
Dear God my father you have known me and loved me
from eternity. You love me with a greater love than I

could ever imagine. I love you in return because you first loved me.

Lord Jesus, my brother, you said, 'Just as I have loved you, you also must love one another.' Let me prove my love for your father and mine by seeing and serving you in all the people I meet today.

In the Evening

FOR A FAMILY (WITH YOUNG CHILDREN).

FATHER, MOTHER OR LEADER: Before we begin to speak with God, we will first try and think of the times today when we have done what he wanted us to do even though it may have been hard. At home (*pause*), at school or work (*pause*), at other times (*pause*).

If we did good deeds today, it is because the Spirit of Jesus guided us to do them and we will thank Him.

GROUP: Spirit of Jesus, we thank you for guiding us today.

LEADER: Now we will think of the times when we didn't do what God wanted. When we didn't behave like brothers and sisters of Jesus. At home (*pause*), at school or work (*pause*), at other times (*pause*). We will tell God our father how sorry we are.

GROUP: Dear God our father we are sorry. Even though you love use very much, we have not always done what you wanted. Because we are sorry please forgive us.

LEADER: We'll now pray for other people

The children can mention individuals or groups as they think fit. For instance:

CHILD: I want to pray for Granny because she is sick.

GROUP: Dear God, please hear our prayers for Granny.

CHILD: I want to pray for children who haven't enough to eat.

GROUP: Dear God, please hear our prayers for children who haven't enough to eat.

If the children are old enough, at this point it may be possible to read a very short excerpt from the Gospel. (One excellent version is New World by Alan Dale.) It is necessary for the leader to say very briefly something about the passage before he reads. For example: 'The part I'm going to read you tells of something Jesus did at the last meal he took with his friends. While we listen, we know that Jesus is asking us to look after and care for each other.' Then John 13, 3–11.

LEADER: Now we say slowly together the prayer that Jesus likes us to pray:

GROUP: Our Father who art in heaven,
hallowed be thy name.
Thy kingdom come, thy will be done,
on earth as it is in heaven,
give us this day our daily bread,
and forgive us our trespasses,
as we forgive those who trespass against us,
and lead us not into temptation,
but deliver us from evil. Amen.

LEADER: We will ask our Lady to pray for us.

GROUP: Hail Mary, full of grace,
the Lord is with thee,
blessed art thou amongst women
and blessed is the fruit of thy womb, Jesus.
Holy Mary, mother of God,
pray for us sinners,
now and at the hour of our death. Amen.

LEADER: The blessing of God, Father, Son and Holy

Spirit be with us all now and stay with us always. Amen.

FOR FAMILY OR GROUP USE, FOR OLDER PEOPLE

LEADER: Let us first of all, in silence, remember our sins. (*Pause.*)

Let us make our confession together.

GROUP: I confess to almighty God,
and to my brothers and sisters,
that I have often sinned
in my thoughts and in my words,
in what I have done
and in what I have failed to do;
and I ask the blessed Mary, ever virgin,
all the angels and saints
and you my brothers and sisters
to pray for me to the Lord our God.

LEADER: May almighty God have mercy on us forgive us our sins

And bring us to everlasting life.

GROUP: Amen.

LEADER: Lord, have mercy   *R.* Lord, have mercy
        Christ, have mercy   *R.* Christ, have mercy
        Lord, have mercy   *R.* Lord, have mercy

LEADER: Now we will listen to God's word.
There follows a reading from the bible. Selections according to the liturgical season are given on pp. 157–185. After the reading:

LEADER: We will pause in silence for a moment and think of the reading and its message for us. (*Pause.*)
Now we will respond to God's word by expressing our faith in him.

GROUP: I believe in God, the Father almighty,
   Creator of heaven and earth
   and in Jesus Christ His only son our Lord
   who was conceived by the Holy Spirit
   born of the virgin Mary
   suffered under Pontius Pilate
   was crucified, dead and buried.
   He descended into hell
   the third day he rose again from the dead.
   He ascended into heaven.
   He sits at the right hand of God the father almighty
   from there he shall come to judge the living and
   the dead.
   I believe in the Holy Spirit
   the holy catholic church
   the communion of saints
   the forgiveness of sins
   the resurrection of the body and life everlasting. Amen.

LEADER: Now we will say one of the prayers Jesus prayed:
   (Ps. 136)
   Give thanks to God, for He is good

GROUP: His love is everlasting

LEADER: Give thanks to the God of gods

GROUP: His love is everlasting

LEADER: Give thanks to the Lord of lords

GROUP: His love is everlasting

LEADER: He alone performs great marvels

GROUP: His love is everlasting

LEADER: His wisdom made the heavens

GROUP: His love is everlasting

LEADER: He set the earth on the waters

GROUP: His love is everlasting

LEADER: He made the great lights

GROUP: His love is everlasting

LEADER: The sun to govern the day

GROUP: His love is everlasting

LEADER: Moon and stars to govern the night

GROUP: His love is everlasting

LEADER: Glory be to the Father
Through the Son,
In the unity of the Holy Spirit

GROUP: As it was in the beginning
Is now and ever shall be
World without end, Amen.

Lord Jesus, our Brother, you said 'where two or three are gathered together in my name there am I in the midst of them'. We are gathered together in your name tonight. We believe that you are really with us now. In your name, we turn to the Father, confident that he will answer our prayers.

Individuals may now make up spontaneous bidding prayers: e.g. 'For the down and outs, sleeping rough and with no one to care for them. . . . Lord hear us – Lord please hear us.'

LEADER: Now we ask Mary to pray for us:

GROUP: Hail, holy queen, mother of mercy,
hail, our life, our sweetness and our hope
to thee do we cry, poor banished children of Eve
to thee do we send up our sighs, mourning and weeping in this vale of tears.
Turn then, most gracious advocate, thine eyes of mercy towards us
And after this our exile, show unto us the blessed fruit of thy womb Jesus

O clement, O loving, O sweet virgin Mary

LEADER: Pray for us, o holy mother of God

GROUP: That we may be made worthy of the promises of Christ

LEADER: Let us pray:
O God, our Father, through the Holy Spirit you prepared the body and soul of the glorious virgin mother, Mary, to be a fit dwelling place for your Son. As we celebrate her memory with joy grant that through her motherly intercession we may be preserved from evil in this world and from eternal death. We make this prayer to you through your Son, Jesus Christ, who lives and reigns with you for ever and ever.

GROUP: Amen.

LEADER: May the Lord lead us when we go,
and help keep us when we sleep
and talk with us when we wake,
and may the peace of God which surpasses all
understanding
keep our hearts and minds
in Christ Jesus our Lord.

GROUP: Amen.

Prayers at Night

FOR USE BY AN INDIVIDUAL

Dear God, my father, here I kneel before you at the end of another day. You are listening to me as if I were the only person alive. You are interested in me, in my work, in my leisure, in my relationships with those around me. You want me to talk to you about my day. . . .

I want to tell you how sorry I am for the times when I did not behave as a son or daughter of yours should,

not only by the things I have done but by the things
I have left undone.

Review of the day may follow

Abba, Father, you are the Lord of all and my Father
too. Even when I am sinning, you still love me. It is I
who when I sin stop loving you. Please forgive me.

Lord Jesus my brother, accept my sorrow for the times
today when by my sins I have damaged our friendship.

O Holy Spirit of Jesus by your mighty power change
my life. By myself I can do no good. If you lead me and
guide me, I can do all things.

It is a deed of kindness to pray for others. Here is a list
of people for whom I may plead: the homeless, the starving,
the sick, the lonely, the despairing, my colleagues at work,
people who are tempted, for people whose marriages are in
danger of breaking up, for those who are mourning a death,
for my friends, and those who wish me good, for those who
dislike me and have tried to harm me.

> *Obviously the list could be much longer. One might pray*
> *for simply one or two groups. It can be difficult to concentrate*
> *on more.*

I have spoken to you, my Father. Now I listen to
what you say to me.

> *Turn now to one of the readings (page 157 following). After*
> *the reading pause for a moment. It may be that you will*
> *be lead to respond to God in your own words.*

And now I ask Mary to pray to God for me.
Hail, Holy Queen, Mother of Mercy,
Hail, our life our sweetness and our hope
To thee do we cry, poor banished children of Eve
To thee do we send up our sighs, mourning and weeping
in this vale of tears.

Turn then, most gracious advocate, thine eyes of mercy
    towards us

And after this our exile, show unto us the blessed fruit
    of thy womb, Jesus

O clement, O loving, O sweet virgin Mary.

Pray for us, O holy Mother of God

That we may be made worthy of the promises of Christ.

O God, our Father, through the Holy Spirit you prepared the body and soul of the glorious virgin mother,
Mary, to be a fit dwelling place for your Son. As we
celebrate her memory with joy grant that through her
motherly intercession we may be preserved from evil in
this world and from eternal death. We make this prayer
to you through your Son, Jesus Christ, who lives and
reigns with you for ever and ever. Amen.

Other Everyday Prayers

The most important happening in human history was when God the Son became a man. Like us he was 'born of a woman'. 'Yes, God loved the world so much that He gave his only Son so that everyone who believes in him may not be lost but may have eternal life.' (John 3, 16–17). We remember this event and thank God when we pray the Angelus.

The Angelus

The angel of the Lord declared unto Mary,
And she conceived by the Holy Spirit.

> Hail Mary ...

Behold the handmaid of the Lord;
Be it done unto me according to thy word.

> Hail Mary ...

And the Word was made flesh
And dwelt amongst us.

> Hail Mary ...

Pray for us, O holy mother of God,
That we may be made worthy of the promises of Christ.

Let us pray.

Pour forth, we beseech Thee, O Lord, Thy grace into our hearts, that we to whom the incarnation of Christ, thy Son, was made known by the message of an angel, may be brought by his passion and cross to the glory of his resurrection, through the same Christ our Lord. Amen.

May the divine assistance remain always with us, and may the souls of the faithful departed through the mercy of God, rest in peace. Amen.

Meal Prayers

Dear God, our Father, please bless both those who have prepared this food and those who are going to eat it. We make this prayer to you through your Son, Jesus Christ, our Lord. Amen.

Thank you, Lord, for your gift to us of the food we have eaten and enjoyed. May our sharing of this meal keep us always united in Christ Jesus, your Son. Amen.

Alternatively:

Bless us, O Lord, and these thy gifts which we are about to receive from thy bounty. Through Christ our Lord. Amen.

We give thee thanks, Almighty God for all thy benefits who livest and reignest for ever and ever. Amen.

A Prayer of Sorrow

I have fallen, Lord, once more.
I can't go on. I'll never succeed
I am ashamed. I don't dare look at you.
And yet I struggled, Lord for I knew you were
　　right near me, bending over me, watching.
But temptation blew like a hurricane
And instead of you I turned my head away
I stepped aside.
While you stood silent and sorrowful . . .

Lord, don't look at me like that.
For I am naked
I am dirty,
I am down, shattered, with no strength left.
I dare make no more promises
I can only stand bowed before you.

'Come, son, look up.
Isn't it mainly your vanity that is wounded?
If you loved me you would grieve but you would trust.
Do you think that there is a limit to God's love?
Do you think that for a moment I stopped loving you?
But you still rely on yourself, son.
You must rely on me.

Ask my pardon
And get up quickly.
You see its not falling that is the worst
But staying on the ground.'

(Michel Quoist, *Prayers of Life*.)

Praying for the Dead

We believe that our journey to the Father which begins when we are born and baptised may continue after death. Who is there so free from human sinfulness and selfishness that when he dies he can be completely and immediately united with the all-holy and all-lovable God? We pray for the dead so as to help them on their way towards God. A prayer that is commonly said is the following. (Psalm 130.)

From the depths I call to you Lord,
Lord listen to my cry for help
Listen compassionately
   to my pleading!
If you never overlooked our sins,
Lord, could anyone survive?
But you do forgive us:
   and for that we revere you.
I wait for the Lord, my soul waits for him,
   I rely on his promise,
   my soul relies on the Lord
   more than a watchman on the coming of dawn.
Let Israel rely on the Lord
   as much as the watchman on the dawn!
For it is with the Lord that mercy is to be found,
and a generous redemption:
it is he who redeemed Israel

from all their sins.
Eternal rest grant to them, O Lord
And let perpetual light shine on them.
May they rest in peace.
Amen.

O Lord hear my prayer,
And let my cry come to you.

O God, the creator and redeemer of all the faithful
Grant to the soul(s) of your departed servant(s) the
remission of all his/her (their) sins that through our
prayers he/she (they) may obtain that pardon which he/
she has (they have) always desired.

   To you, O Lord, we commend the soul of your servant
(*name*). He/she is dead to this world. May he/she live to
you. And whatever sins he/she may have committed in
this life do you in your most merciful goodness forgive.
Lord Jesus you are the resurrection and the Life. You
comforted Martha and Mary on the death of their
brother. Console now those who are sad at the death of
(*name*) our brother/sister.

Holy Spirit of God, by your power Jesus was raised to
life again. We also look forward to that day of our own
resurrection when we shall all be united once more with
those we love in the unending happiness of heaven.

We make these prayers in and through Jesus Christ who
lives and reigns united to you by the Holy Spirit, for
ever and ever. Amen.

Praying to God
Our Father

Prayer is directed to the Father through Jesus in the Holy Spirit. This is the way Jesus told us to pray. 'You should pray like this, Our Father, who art in heaven . . .' *(Matthew 6, 9). 'I tell you most solemnly, anything you ask from the Father, he will grant to you in my name' (John 16, 23).*

When we read, in the Gospel of Jesus praying, it is with the Father that he is talking. He is not praying simply to give us a good example. He needed to pray.

Most of the prayers in the Church's prayerbook, the Missal, are to the Father 'through Jesus Christ, Our Lord'. Perhaps the most important is the one which comes at the end of the Eucharastic prayer:

> Through him,
> with him,
> in him,
> in the unity of the Holy Spirit,
> all glory and honour is yours,
> almighty Father,
> for ever and ever. Amen.

This would be an excellent prayer to say even apart from Mass.

The Lord's prayer is so called because it was given to us by Our Lord, Jesus Christ. We are so familiar with it that we tend to say it quickly and possibly without much thought. It is good from time to time to say it very slowly, pausing after each phrase:

OUR FATHER. Yes Lord, you really are my Father. You care for me deeply. Because you are my Father and I am your child, I trust myself completely to you. You can look after me so much better than I can myself.

HALLOWED BE THY NAME. Dear Father you are so good, you are all holy, you are perfect. I adore you. I pray that all men may worship you.

THY KINGDOM COME. Your kingdom will come in its fullness at the end. But I must now work and pray for its coming. Every prayer I say, every work I do, to make the world a better place, is bringing on the day when your Son will hand this world over to you.

THY WILL BE DONE. Dear Father I am not praying so that you will do what I want, but so that I will learn to do what you want. 'Not my will but thine be done.'

GIVE US THIS OUR DAILY BREAD – and not only us, but those who live in countries where food is always scarce.

AND FORGIVE US OUR TRESPASSES. Forgive me my sins, O Lord God, because I am truly sorry.

AS WE FORGIVE THOSE WHO TRESPASS AGAINST US. Help me to forgive those who hurt me. Help me to show love to all who offend me.

AND LEAD US NOT INTO TEMPTATION. Hardly an hour passes, dear Father, when I am not tempted to do something which I know you would not want me to do. Help me to stay true to you.

BUT DELIVER US FROM EVIL. All sorts of evil – being a slave to myself rather than being a son to you, feeling that I do not need you, forgetfulness of others' needs. . . .

O God, our Father, you have loved us with an everlasting love and in your mercy you have prepared for those who love you in return, joy that is beyond our understanding. Pour into our hearts such a sense of your love that loving you above all things we may obtain your promises which exceed all that we can desire. We make this prayer to you through Jesus Christ Our Lord. Amen.

Praise and Gratitude

A Christian is one who goes through life praising and thanking God, his Father, for all the wonderful things He has done for him. This praising and thanking reaches its climax in the Holy Eucharist. The word 'Eucharist' means 'remembering all God's kind acts and thanking Him' with Jesus.

Every day we come across so many good things and we should thank God for them: the joy of buying something new, the smell of cooking, a letter from an old friend, the smile of a grateful person, the bewitching look on the face of a child, the feeling of satisfaction after a job well done. We can make our own prayers of gratitude for all these things as we come across them.

The Church has a very ancient and solemn prayer of praise and thanksgiving. Its name comes from its first two Latin words.

Te Deum

We praise you, O God, we acknowledge you as Lord and master.
Eternal Father, the whole world adores you.
All the angels sing your praise.

The Powers of heaven, the Cherubim and Seraphim, all proclaim your glory saying, holy, holy, holy is the Lord God of angels.

Heaven and earth are filled with your majestic glory.

The renowned company of the apostles, the praise-worthy band of prophets, the white-robed army of martyrs, all these praise you.

The Church too, throughout the world, proclaims her faith in you: Father of limitless majesty, your only Son who is to be adored, your Holy Spirit, our advocate.

O Christ, you are the king of glory. You are the Father's eternal Son. In order to set us free, you did not shrink from being conceived in the womb of a virgin.

When you had destroyed death's sting, you opened up to believers the kingdom of heaven.

Now you are at the right hand of God, in the glory of the Father.

You will one day come as our judge.

Therefore we beg you now to aid your servants whom you have redeemed with your precious blood.

Make it that they be numbered with your saints in eternal glory.

Bring your people to safety. Bless those who belong to you.

Be their ruler and their support for ever.

Each day of our lives we praise you.

We want your name hallowed now and for ever.

In your mercy, Lord, grant that through this day we be kept free from sin.

Have mercy on us O Lord, have mercy.

Because we have put our hope in you, let your mercy enfold us.

I have put all my hope in you, Lord. Let me never be dismayed.

Jesus Prays to His Father

Jesus prayed to his Father and 'still makes inter-cession for us'. He loved his Father above all and He spoke with his Father in his own words. Some-times, however, he prayed the psalms. These are the folk-like songs the Hebrews sang or said and they are found in the Bible. Jesus knew them all off by heart and for this reason, the book of psalms has been called 'Jesus' prayerbook'. When he was on the cross, he prayed one of these psalms, 'My God, my God, why have you deserted me?'. This is Psalm 22 and although it begins in this way, it ends on a note of trust in God's victory. Here is part of a prayer-psalm that Jesus prayed. (Psalm 139.) In this prayer we tell God our Father that we believe he is near us wherever we go. As you will see, an astronaut could well say this prayer.

Lord, you examine me and know me,
you know if I am standing or sitting,
you read my thoughts from far away,
whether I walk or lie down, you are watching,
you know every detail of my conduct.

The word is not even on my tongue,
Lord, before you know all about it;
close behind and close in front you hold me,
shielding me with your hand.

Such insight is too wonderful to grasp,
a height to which my mind cannot aspire.

Where could I go to escape your spirit?
Where could I flee from your presence?
If I probe the outer space, you are there,
if I lie down in the grave, you are there too.

Were I to fly to the point of sunrise
or westwards across the sea,
your hand would still be guiding me,
your right hand holding on to me.
If I chose to live in perpetual night,
in a darkness excluding all light,
that darkness would not be dark to you;
for you, that night would be as light as day.

Since you yourself have created my very being
and put me together in my mother's womb,
in wonder I thank you for making me;
how mysterious, like everything you make!

You know me through and through,
from having watched my bones take shape
when I was being assembled in secret,
stitched together in the darkness of the womb.

God, examine my heart, to see what I love,
Analyse my mind, to see what I think;
Make sure I am not likely to offend you,
And guide me on the path that is eternal.

Praying to
Jesus Christ

As we have seen, most of our prayers should be to the Father through Jesus in the Holy Spirit. Nevertheless we should also speak to Jesus since 'he is the image of the unseen God' (Colossians 1, 15). As we pray we can make a picture of him in our minds, something we cannot do so easily of God the Father. He will listen to us and gently join our prayers with his to the Father. Here are some prayers to Jesus that Christians have found helpful. Begin by telling Jesus you believe he is with you and listening to you as truly as he listened to Peter and the apostles when he walked the roads of Palestine with them.

Jesus Christ,
Close beside me here and now
yesterday, today and the same forever
the same now as with Mary in Nazareth
the same as with Peter in Galilee
the same as with Magdalen in Bethany.
You will not force yourself upon me
waiting for me to make the first step
waiting till I in turn ask you to come.
Jesus Christ
Jesus, Lord of all,
Christ, the Son of the Living God.

To whom shall we go?
You have the words of Eternal Life
    I believe in you
    I love you
    I trust you
    I want you
    I give myself to you
    give yourself to me.
    Come Lord Jesus, come quickly.

                      (Archbishop Goodier)

O Lord Jesus Christ,
    take as your right
    receive as my gift
    all my liberty
my memory, my understanding, my will
    all that I have
    all that I am
    all that I can be.
To you, O Lord, I restore it,
    all is yours,
dispose of it according to your will
    give me your love
    give me your grace
    it is enough for me.

                          (St Ignatius)

Thanks be to you, my Lord Jesus Christ
for all the benefits which you have given me
for all the pains and insults which you have borne for me.
O most merciful redeemer, friend and brother
may I know you more clearly
love you more dearly
and serve you more nearly. Amen.

                          (St Richard)

Christ with me, Christ before me
Christ behind me, Christ in me,
Christ beneath me, Christ above me,
Christ on my right, Christ on my left,
Christ where I lie, Christ where I sit,
Christ where I arise,
Christ in the heart of every man who thinks of me,
Christ in the mouth of every man who speaks of me
Christ in every eye that sees me
Christ in every ear that hears me
Salvation is of the Lord,
Salvation is of Christ,
May your salvation, Lord be ever with us.

(St Patrick)

The Sacred Heart

The heart is the symbol of love. People say 'I love you with all my heart'. When we speak of the Sacred Heart of Jesus, we are thinking of the great love the Father has shown us through his divine Son, the truly human Jesus, 'like to us in everything except sin'.

Heart of Jesus, truly human, have mercy on us
heart of Jesus, truly divine
heart of Jesus still praying for us to the Father
heart of Jesus in all things like to us except sin
heart of Jesus loving your friends to the end
heart of Jesus whose love for men is scorned by many
heart of Jesus, my hope in sadness
heart of Jesus, my strength in temptation
heart of Jesus, my protection in danger
heart of Jesus, loving me now despite everything

Almighty and everlasting God,
look upon the heart of your beloved Son
and upon the praise and satisfaction
he offered you on behalf of sinners.
Forgive those who now seek your mercy
in the name of the same Jesus Christ, your Son
who lives and reigns with you for ever and ever. Amen.

A Visit to Church

While we are trying to do what his Father wants us to do, Jesus is really with us always united to us by His Spirit. We can turn to him at any time and in any place, sure that He is listening to us.

Nevertheless the focal point of his presence is the Blessed Sacrament. Just as God by the pillar of fire gave a sign of His presence to the Hebrew people on their journey to the promised land (Exodus 13, 22), so the presence of God in Jesus is signified by the 'fire' of the lamp that burns in our churches. It points to the special presence of Jesus in this sacrament, the Blessed Sacrament. We are on the difficult journey through life to the promised land of heaven and we come to church to renew the dedication we make of our lives with Jesus to the Father whenever we celebrate the eucharist at Mass.

When we are at Mass we are aware that we are a family celebrating together. The prayers are fixed and said aloud.

Coming to church on our own, outside of Mass time, we have the opportunity of talking more as individuals, perhaps more personally and intimately, with Jesus.

There are a variety of different ways in which you may 'make a visit'. Three suggestions are here offered.

A Conversation Visit

Begin by making a vivid picture of Jesus in your mind. The best prayer will be the conversation you hold with him in your own words, exactly as if he were visible to you. Tell him about yourself, your fears, your hopes, your worries, what has happened to you. But also talk to him of the needs of others:

> *the sick, the dying, the dead,*
> *the tempted, the sinners,*
> *your family,*
> *your colleagues at work or school,*
> *those you love, those you dislike . . .*
> > *and so on.*

Before leaving, listen to what he may have to tell you. 'Speak Lord, your servant is listening'

(Samuel 3, 9).

A Programmed Visit

You may prefer something more formal. Here is a programme of prayer. The prayers given here are no more than suggested outlines. It would be better for you to make up your own.

FAITH Lord Jesus, I believe that you are near me. You are listening to what I say.

ADORATION Lord Jesus, I adore you. You are my Lord and my God.

UNION Lord Jesus, I want to love you and to be your close friend. You proved your love for me by dying for me. Let me prove my love for you by caring for all the people I meet.

THANKS Lord Jesus, thank you for all you have done for me.

SORROW Lord Jesus, forgive me for the times I have let you down. I am very sorry. I shall try to stay true to you.

Conclude as in the previous set of prayers by remembering the needs of others.

A Visit based on the Mass

In this visit to church, you may follow the order of Mass. You may begin, as at Mass, with the liturgy of the Word, that is, you read a passage from the Bible or one of the readings given on pages 158 – 187. After the reading you ponder on what you have read and see if you can discover what it is God is wanting you to take from it. Then you express your assent to God's word, either in your own words, or through one of the Creeds (see pages 18 and 100).

At this point you may make up your own bidding prayers for people in need – the sick, the homeless, the workless, the hungry, those at war, the needs of God's church, the whole family of God – the bishop, the priests of this church, the parishioners.

Next offer your work, your joys, your sorrows, to the Father (the offertory). You beg Jesus to change yourself into someone more like him and with him you offer yourself to the Father (the consecration). You ask Jesus to give himself to you. You need him. By this spiritual union you express your love, not only towards him, but to everyone (the communion). You ask God to bless you, Father Son and Spirit, as you take your leave.

You may also wish to say one of the eucharistic prayers (see pages 107, 111, 114, and 118).

The Holy Spirit

The Holy Spirit unites the Father and the Son *in their love for each other. Our Mass prayers usually end in this way: 'Through Jesus Christ, our Lord, who lives and reigns with you,* in the unity of the Holy Spirit, *world without end. Amen.' The Holy Spirit* unites us to Jesus. *When we pray to the Father, Jesus prays with us because he is united to us by His Spirit. 'The Spirit you received is not the spirit of slaves bringing fear into your lives again; it is the Spirit of his Son and it makes us cry out, Abba, Father'* (Galatians 4, 6). *Abba is the Hebrew equivalent of 'Daddy' expressing the intimate relationship that should exist between God and His children.*

The Holy Spirit unites us to each other. *It was the Spirit of pride that disunited the people of Babel who could not understand each other* (see Genesis 11). *It was the Holy Spirit who so united the people on Pentecost Sunday though they spoke different languages they all were united in understanding what the apostles said. In the Mass we pray: 'May all of us who share in the body and blood of Christ be brought together in unity by the Holy Spirit'. 'Grant that we who are nourished by His body and blood may be filled with his Holy Spirit, and become one body, one spirit in Christ'.*

Here are two prayers to the Holy Spirit frequently used:

Come O Holy Spirit, fill the hearts of your faithful and
    kindle in them the fire of your love.
Send forth your Spirit
And they shall be created
And you will renew the face of the earth.

O God, our Father, you teach your family through the
    light of your Holy Spirit. Grant that by the same Spirit
    we may be truly wise, and always rejoice in his con-
    solation, through Christ, our Lord, Amen.

*There are two very ancient Latin hymns to the Holy
Spirit. The following versions are free translations
in prose form. Both these hymns in poetic form can
be found in most hymn books. (See also p. 72.)*

O Creator Spirit of God, come to those
    who belong to you; and fill them with your grace.
You are called 'the helper' 'the Father's gift' 'the living
    spring' a 'fire' 'a spiritual comfort'.

You give us your aid in seven different ways, for you are
    the power of God, promised by him, to help us speak
    and pray.

Enlighten our minds, warm our hearts, and with your
    power strengthen our weakness.

Keep our enemy away from us. Give us peace, so that
    with you as our guide, we may be delivered from all
    that is evil.

We pray that through you we may know the Father
    and Son.
We believe that you are the Spirit of love uniting them.
Glory be to the Father, and to the Son, who rose from
    the dead, and to you, our helper, for ever and ever.
    Amen.

Come, O Holy Spirit, and shine on us the rays of your
  light.
You are a father to the poor. Come, then,
  giver of presents, come to us, you who
  are the light of men's minds.
You are the best of all friends, a man's gracious
  guest and companion.
You offer rest to those who labour, shelter to
  those who look for shade,
  comfort to those who are sad.
O blessed light, fill the hearts of all christians.
Without you a man is an empty shell,
  unable to do any good.
Wash away whatever is unclean in man,
  refresh whatever is parched,
  heal whatever is wounded
  soften whatever is unyielding
  warm whatever is cold
  rule whatever is unruly.
Give your seven gifts to all those who rely on you.
Give them the reward of good living,
  salvation and joy for ever. Amen.

Listening to the Holy Spirit

*We speak of 'listening to the Holy Spirit'. 'Doing
what the Spirit of Jesus tells us.'*

*This does not mean that we hear his voice whisper
physically in our ears. The Spirit of Jesus speaks to
us in various ways. You may remember that he
appeared to the apostles as fire and wind.*

*Sometimes when we listen to the advice of a friend,
it may be that the Holy Spirit is telling us what to
do. If we see someone in misfortune and we feel com-*

pelled to help, it is the Spirit who is speaking to us. An odd word said over the radio or T.V., a paragraph in a book, an advert in a newspaper – the Spirit of Jesus may be invading our lives in all these different ways.

But if our lives are to be guided by the Spirit, then we must be listening people.

Our Lady

Jesus was born of Mary. Jesus is God. This is why the Council of Ephesus (431) declared that Mary is rightly to be called the Mother of God. Throughout the centuries most christians have felt that Mary was worthy of special honour because of her closeness to Jesus. 'Near the cross of Jesus stood his mother ... Seeing his mother and the disciple he loved standing near her, Jesus said to his mother, "Woman, this is your son." Then to the disciple he said "This is your mother" and from that moment the disciple made a place for her in his home' (John 19, 25).

Many people have concluded from this Gospel incident that Jesus was appointing Mary to be a mother not only of his friend John, but of all men. And so it is that we pray to Mary. Perhaps it would be more correct to say that we ask Mary to pray for us; strictly speaking, God, Father, Son and Spirit, are the only persons to whom we pray directly as the source of all good.

Many phrases of the Hail Mary are taken from the Gospel of St Luke.

Hail Mary ('Rejoice')
Full of grace ('so highly favoured')
The Lord is with thee ('the Lord is with you')
Blessed art thou among women ('You are the happiest of women')

And blessed is the fruit of thy womb, Jesus ('And happy
    too is your Son')

Holy Mary, Mother of God,
Pray for us sinners,
Now and at the hour of our death. Amen.

The Rosary

*Each section or 'decade' of the Rosary consists of one
Our Father, ten Hail Marys, one Glory be to the
Father (there could be less than ten Hail Marys if
ten proved too long.) While we say the Hail Mary
we picture in our minds one of the great happenings
in our salvation. In other words the Hail Marys act
as a timing device (lasting about a minute and a
half).*

Here are the fifteen mysteries:

The Annunciation: Mary is asked to be the Mother of
    God. She replies 'I am the handmaid of the Lord. Let
    what you have said be done to me' (Luke 1, 38).

The Visitation: Mary goes to help her cousin Elizabeth
    who is also expecting a baby (Luke 1, 42).

The Birth of Our Lord: Far from home, and in a shelter
    built for cattle, Mary gives birth to her child (Luke 2).

The Presentation in the Temple: Mary and Joseph offer
    their child to God (Luke 2).

The Finding of Jesus in the Temple: Jesus, now aged 12,
    was lost but is found again. 'His mother stored up
    all these things in her heart' (Luke 2, 52).

The Agony in the Garden: Jesus suffered from fear and
    sadness on the night he was betrayed (Luke 22, 39).

Jesus is scourged: Jesus is ordered to be flogged in an

attempt by Pilate to placate those who wanted his death (Luke 23, 15).

Jesus is Crowned with Thorns: The soldiers mock Jesus in this painful way (Mark 15, 16.)

Jesus Carries his Cross: The innocent one is condemned as a criminal to carry his own cross (Luke 23, 26).

Jesus Dies on the Cross: After three hours of pain Jesus cries out 'Father, unto your hands I commit my Spirit', and dies (Luke 23, 46).

Jesus Rises Again: After three days in the tomb, the Father raised Jesus to life again (Acts 3, 15).

Jesus Goes to His Father: The Ascension: Jesus withdrew his visible presence from us. But he never leaves us (Acts 1).

Jesus Sends his Spirit: He had said before he died 'I shall send you a comforter'. This Holy Spirit transformed the apostles on Whit Sunday (Acts 2).

His Mother is taken up into heaven: His mother is no longer seen by us but she is not far away. She prays for us.

Jesus honours His Mother: He rewards her for her faith and loyalty by making her queen of the universe.

Here is another prayer in which we ask Mary to pray for us:

Remember, O most loving virgin Mary,
that is it a thing unheard of
that anyone ever had recourse to your protection
implored your help or sought your intercession
and was left forsaken.
Filled therefore with confidence
I fly to you, O Mother, virgin of virgins,
to you I come, before you stand, a sorrowful sinner.

Despise not my words, O Mother of the Word,
but hear and grant my prayer. Amen.

Litany of Our Lady

Lord have mercy
Lord have mercy
Christ have mercy
Christ have mercy
Lord have mercy
Lord have mercy
Christ hear us
Christ graciously hear us
God the Father of heaven have mercy on us
God the Son, redeemer of the world have mercy on us
God the Holy Spirit, have mercy on us
Holy Trinity, one God, have mercy on us
Holy Mary, pray for us (*this response is repeated*)
Holy mother of God
Holy virgin of virgins
Mother of Christ
Mother of divine grace
Mother most pure
Mother most chaste
Mother inviolate
Mother undefiled
Mother most lovable
Mother most admirable
Mother of good counsel
Mother of our creator
Mother of our saviour
Virgin most prudent
Virgin most venerable
Virgin most renowned
Virgin most powerful

Virgin most merciful
Virgin most faithful
Mirror of justice
Seat of wisdom
Cause of our joy
Spiritual vessel
Vessel of honour
Singular vessel of devotion
Mystical rose
Tower of David
Tower of ivory
House of gold
Ark of the covenant
Gate of heaven
Morning star
Health of the sick
Refuge of sinners
Comfort of the afflicted
Help of christians
Queen of angels
Queen of patriarchs
Queen of prophets
Queen of apostles
Queen of martyrs
Queen of confessors
Queen of virgins
Queen of all saints
Queen conceived without original sin
Queen assumed into heaven
Queen of the most holy Rosary
Queen of peace

Lamb of God, you take away the sins of the world, spare
us O Lord.

Lamb of God, you take away the sins of the world,
   graciously hear us O Lord,

Lamb of God, you take away the sins of the world, have
   mercy on us.

   Pray for us, O holy mother of God,

That we may be made worthy of the promises of Christ.

Let us pray: Grant that we your servants Lord, may
   enjoy unfailing health of mind and body and through
   the prayers of the ever blessed virgin Mary in her
   glory, free us from our sorrows in this world and give
   us eternal happiness in the next. We make this prayer
   to you through Christ, our Lord. Amen.

   Here is Mary's own prayer, the 'Magnificat' (See
   Luke 2, 46):

My soul proclaims the greatness of the Lord

and my spirit exults in God my Saviour;

because he has looked upon his lowly handmaid.

Yes, from this day forward all generations will call be
   blessed,

for the Almighty has done great things for me.

Holy is his name,

and his mercy reaches from age to age for those who
   fear him.

He has shown the power of his arm,

he has routed the proud of heart.

He has pulled down princes from their thrones and
   exalted the lowly.

The hungry he has filled with good things, the rich sent
   empty away.

He has come to the help of Israel his servant, mindful
   of his mercy

– according to the promise he made to our ancestors –

of his mercy to Abraham and to his descendants for ever.

The Saints

Just as I may ask an acquaintance or a friend to pray for me, so I may ask one of the Saints. Together with the saints we are all members of God's family. This is partly expressed by the phrase 'Communion of Saints'.

The Church's prayer-book, the missal, asks us to use the litany of the Saints on certain important occasions, for example at the paschal vigil (the most important Mass of the year), and at the ordination and consecration of priests and bishops.

Here is a prayer asking all the saints to pray for us.

May Christ make us an everlasting gift to you, heavenly Father,
and enable us to share in the inheritance of your saints,
with Mary, the virgin mother of God;
with the apostles, the martyrs,
saint . . . (the saint of the day)
and all your saints,
on whose constant intercession we rely for help.

A person may well want to ask the Saint after whom he has been named, to pray for him.

Prayers During Illness

Father, I find it hard to accept this illness.
I am impatient.
I find it hard to speak to anyone.
I find it hard to talk to you.
I am wrapped up in pity and worry for myself.
I worry over my health
I worry about the things I would like to do, ought to
    do, but now I can't.
At a time like this I find it hard
    to believe in you
    to trust in you
    to love you
And yet I want to believe, to trust, to love.
I know you really care for me.
I cast all my care upon you.
I leave myself entirely in your kind hands.
Not my will but yours be done.

*St Paul wrote: 'It makes me happy to suffer for you
(Christians at Colossae) as I am suffering now, and in my
own body to do what I can to make up all that has still to
be undergone by Christ for the sake of his body, the Church'
(Colossians 1, 24). He speaks as though Jesus left us an
opportunity to join our sufferings to his for the redemption
of the world.*

Lord Jesus, I think of the pains you endured for me. The great sadness of the garden, your scourging and crowning, your cross, your death. You had to suffer to enter into your glory. The sufferings of this time are not to be compared to the glory that is to come. In the strength of your Spirit I join my sufferings to yours for the redemption of the world.

Lord Jesus Christ, Son of God, have mercy on me a sinner.

Prayer
for Unity

O God, our Father,
you are Father of all men equally
Father of Christians and Jews
of whites and blacks
(and all those in between)
Father of those who believe in you
and equally of those who don't.
Send your Holy Spirit, the Spirit who unites people,
so that all men will forget their differences,
put aside their prejudices
and work together for the good of all
no matter what their creed
no matter what their colour
so that at the end
this world, perfected by men co-operating together
and co-operating with you
may be handed over to you by your beloved Son.

Unite especially those who believe in your Son
all Christians, Catholic, Orthodox and Protestant
(and all those in between)
break down the divisions between Christians
so that soon all may be united again
and once more be one family around your table.

Still more do we pray you,
to unite more closely those of our Faith,

those who love only change and those who love only
   traditions
(and all those in between)
so that the people of your Pilgrim Church
led by the Spirit towards your Kingdom
may work, pray and live happily together
in charity and in peace.

Part Two

MEETING JESUS NOW:
THE SACRAMENTS

Jesus said, 'Know that I am with you always; yes, to the end of time'. He said these words on Ascension Day, and so we should not think that on this day Jesus left us. What he did on this day was to withdraw his visible *presence. We cannot see him but he is as present to us now as he was to his friends in Palestine. He is present to us through his Spirit who unites us to him.*

He is close to those who try always to do what his Father wants. 'Anyone who does the will of my Father in Heaven, he is my brother and sister and mother.'

He is among Christians who meet together. 'Where two or three meet in my name, I shall be there with them.'

We hear his voice when the Bible is read in church.

We meet him each time one of the seven sacraments is celebrated. The sacrament of his special presence is the Holy Eucharist. Here he is present in the appearance of food and drink: bread and wine. 'Anyone who does eat my flesh and drink my blood has eternal life, and I shall raise him up on the last day.'

When Jesus was in Palestine he was able to do things only for people who had faith in him. 'Your faith deserves it, so let this be done for you.' 'Your faith has saved you, go in peace.'

In Nazareth, his home town, he was able to help no one because the people of Nazareth had no faith in him. It is the same today. If we don't bring faith with us when we celebrate the sacraments, he will hardly be able to help us. In his meetings now with people through the signs we call sacraments, our Lord Jesus first asks for our faith, and in proportion to our faith, he is able to help us.

We talk about the sacraments as 'celebrations'. What is a celebration? A happy happening that takes place among friends. And so it is with the sacraments. We are not alone when we celebrate the sacraments – it is not just the priest, Jesus, and me. There are always other members of God's family involved – as we shall see.

Baptism

The most important day of my life was the day on which I was baptised. On that day I was made a son or daughter of God my Father. Jesus became my brother, united to me through his Holy Spirit.

I was also accepted as a member of God's family – the Church.

It is likely that at the time of my baptism I was too young to know what was happening, but now that I am older I am able to live out my baptism every day, by trying to live like a true son or daughter of God.

Entrance Song

A suitable hymn or psalm, e.g. – Psalm 22

The Lord is my shepherd; there is nothing I shall want.

Fresh and green are the pastures where he gives me repose.

Near restful waters he leads me, to revive my fainting spirit.

He guides me along the right path; he is true to his name.

If I should walk in the valley of darkness, no evil would I fear.

You are there with your crook and your staff; with these you give me comfort.

You have prepared a banquet for me in the sight of my
foes.

My head you have anointed with oil; my cup is over-
flowing.

Surely goodness and kindness shall follow me all the
days of my life.

In the Lord's own house shall I dwell for ever and ever.

Reception of the Children

*The Celebrant greets all present; especially the parents and
godparents, reminding them briefly of the joy with which
the parents welcomed their children as gifts from God, the
source of life, who now wishes to bestow his own life on these
little ones. Then he questions the parents of each child:*

CELEBRANT: What name have you given your child (each
of these children)?

PARENTS: *N.* . . .

CELEBRANT: What do you ask of God's Church for *N.* . . .
(these children)?

PARENTS: Baptism.

CELEBRANT (*in these or similar terms*): You have asked to
have your child (children) baptised. In doing so you
are accepting the responsibility of training them in the
practice of the faith. It will be your duty to bring them
up to keep God's commandments as Christ taught
us, by loving God and our neighbour. Do you clearly
understand what you are undertaking?

PARENTS: We do.

CELEBRANT (*addressing the godparents in these or similar
words*): Are you ready to help these parents in their
duty as Christian mothers and fathers?

GODPARENTS: We are.

CELEBRANT: *N....* (My dear children), the Christian community welcomes you with great joy. In its name I claim you for Christ our Saviour by the sign of his cross.

I now trace the cross on your foreheads, and invite your parents and godparents to do the same.

He signs each child on the forehead, in silence. Then he invites the parents and godparents to do the same.

The Celebration of God's Word

One or two of the following gospel passages are read; all may sit.

John 3, 1–6 *The meeting with Nicodemus.*
Matthew 28, 18–20 *The Apostles are sent to preach and baptise.*
Mark 1, 9–11 *The Baptism of Jesus*
Mark 10, 13–16 *'Let the little children come to me.'*

After the reading the Celebrant gives a short homily. This may be followed by a period of silence and a suitable hymn.

INTERCESSIONS (PRAYER OF THE FAITHFUL)

CELEBRANT: Dear brethren, let us ask our Lord Jesus Christ to look lovingly on this child (these children) who are to be baptised, on his/her (their) parents and godparents, and on the baptised.

READER: By the mystery of your death and resurrection, bathe this child (these children) in light, give him/her (them) the new life of baptism and welcome him/her (them) into your holy Church. Lord, hear us.

ALL: Lord, graciously hear us.

READER: Through baptism and confirmation, make him/her (them) your faithful follower(s) and witness(es) to your gospel. Lord, hear us.

ALL: Lord, graciously hear us.

READER: Lead him/her (them) by a holy life to the joys of God's kingdom. Lord, hear us.

ALL: Lord, graciously hear us.

READER: Make the lives of his/her (their) parents and godparents examples of faith to inspire this child (these children). Lord, hear us.

ALL: Lord, graciously hear us.

READER: Keep his/her family (their families) always in your love. Lord, hear us.

ALL: Lord, graciously hear us.

READER: Renew the grace of our baptism in each one of us. Lord, hear us.

ALL: Lord, graciously hear us.

The Celebrant invites all present to invoke the saints

Holy Mary, Mother of God	pray for us
Saint John the Baptist,	pray for us
Saint Joseph	pray for us
Saint Peter and Saint Paul	pray for us

The names of other saints may be added, especially the patrons of the children to be baptised, and of the church or locality. The litany concludes:

All you saints of God	pray for us

Prayer of Exorcism and Anointing before Baptism

CELEBRANT: Almighty and ever-living God,
you sent your only Son into the world
to cast out the power of Satan, spirit of evil,
to rescue man from the kingdom of darkness,
and bring him into the splendour of your kingdom of light.

We pray for this child (these children):
set him/her (them) free from original sin,
make him/her (them) temples of your glory,
and send your Holy Spirit to dwell within him/her
   (them).
(We ask this) through Christ our Lord.

ALL: Amen.

CELEBRANT: We anoint you with the oil of salvation
   in the name of Christ our Saviour;
   may he strengthen you
   with his power,
   who lives and reigns for ever and ever.

ALL: Amen.

*He anoints each child on the breast with the oil of cate-
chumens*

The Celebration of the Sacrament

*All proceed to the baptistery. At the font the celebrant
briefly reminds the people of the wonderful work of God
whose plan it is to sanctify man, body and soul, through
water. He may use the following or similar words:*

CELEBRANT: My dear brethren, now we ask God to give
   this child (these children) new life in abundance
   through water and the Holy Spirit.

BLESSING AND INVOCATION OF GOD OVER THE BAPTISMAL WATER

CELEBRANT: Father, you give us grace through sacramental signs, which tell us of the wonders of your
   unseen power.

   In baptism we use your gift of water, which you
   have made a rich symbol of the grace you give us in
   this sacrament.

   At the very dawn of creation your Spirit breathed

on the waters, making them the wellspring of all holiness.

The waters of the great flood you made a sign of the waters of baptism, that make an end of sin and a new beginning of goodness.

Through the waters of the Red Sea you led Israel out of slavery, to be an image of God's holy people, set free from sin by baptism.

In the waters of the Jordan your Son was baptised by John and anointed with the Spirit.

Your Son willed that water and blood should flow from his side as he hung upon the cross.

After his resurrection he told his disciples: 'Go out and teach all nations, baptising them in the name of the Father, and of the Son, and of the Holy Spirit.'

Father, look now with love upon your Church, and unseal for her the fountain of baptism.

By the power of the Spirit give to the water of this font the grace of your Son.

You created man in your own likeness: cleanse him from sin in a new birth to innocence by water and the Spirit.

He touches the water with his right hand and continues:

We ask you, Father, with your Son to send the Holy Spirit upon the water of this font. May all who are buried with Christ in the death of baptism rise also with him to newness of life. (We ask this) through Christ our Lord.

ALL: Amen.

RENUNCIATION OF SIN AND PROFESSION OF FAITH

CELEBRANT: Dear parents and godparents, you have come here to present this child (these children) for baptism. By water and the Holy Spirit they are to receive the gift of new life from God, who is love.

On your part, you must make it your constant care to bring them up in the practice of the faith. See that the divine life which God gives them is kept safe from the poison of sin, to grow always stronger in their hearts.

If your faith makes you ready to accept this responsibility, renew now the vows of your own baptism. Reject sin; profess your faith in Christ Jesus. This is the faith of the Church. This is the faith in which this child is (these children are) about to be baptised. Do you reject Satan?

PARENTS & GODPARENTS: I do.

CELEBRANT: And all his works?

PARENTS & GODPARENTS: I do.

CELEBRANT: And all his empty promises?

PARENTS & GODPARENTS: I do.

CELEBRANT: Do you believe in God, the Father almighty, creator of heaven and earth?

PARENTS & GODPARENTS: I do.

CELEBRANT: Do you believe in Jesus Christ, his only Son, our Lord, who was born of the Virgin Mary, was crucified, died, and was buried, rose from the dead, and is now seated at the right hand of the Father?

PARENTS & GODPARENTS: I do.

CELEBRANT: Do you believe in the Holy Spirit, the holy catholic Church, the communion of saints, the forgiveness of sins, the resurrection of the body, and life everlasting?

PARENTS & GODPARENTS: I do.

CELEBRANT: This is our faith. This is the faith of the Church. We are proud to profess it, in Christ Jesus our Lord.

ALL: Amen.

BAPTISM

CELEBRANT: Is it your will that *N.* should be baptised in the faith of the Church, which we have all professed with you?

PARENTS & GODPARENTS: It is.

The Celebrant pours water over the child's head three times, saying:

CELEBRANT: *N.,* I baptise you in the name of the Father, and of the Son, and of the Holy Spirit.

ANOINTING WITH CHRISM

CELEBRANT: God the Father of our Lord Jesus Christ has freed you from sin, given you a new birth by water and the Holy Spirit, and welcomed you into his holy people. He now anoints you with the chrism of salvation. As Christ was anointed Priest, Prophet, and King, so may you live always as members of his body, sharing everlasting life.

ALL: Amen.

The Celebrant anoints each child on the crown of the head with sacred chrism, without saying anything.

CLOTHING WITH WHITE GARMENT

CELEBRANT: *N.,* you have become a new creation, and have clothed yourself in Christ. See in this white garment the outward sign of your Christian dignity. With your family and friends to help you by word and example, bring that dignity unstained into the everlasting life of heaven.

ALL: Amen.

The white garments are put on the children.

THE LIGHTED CANDLE

The Celebrant takes the Easter candle and says:

CELEBRANT: Receive the light of Christ.

Someone from each family (e.g. the father or godfather) lights the child's candle from the Easter candle.

Parents and godparents, this light is entrusted to you to be kept burning brightly. This child (these children) of yours has been enlightened by Christ. He/she is to walk always as a child of the light. May he/she keep the flame of faith alive in his/her (their) heart. When the Lord comes, may he/she (they) go out to meet him with all the saints in the heavenly kingdom.

THE EPHPHETHA

The Celebrant touches the ears and mouth of each child with his thumb, saying:

CELEBRANT: The Lord Jesus made the deaf hear and the dumb speak. May he soon touch your ears to receive his word, and your mouth to proclaim his faith, to the praise and glory of God the Father.

ALL: Amen.

Conclusion of the Rite

They proceed to the altar, unless the baptism was performed in the sanctuary. The lighted candles are carried for the children. A suitable hymn may be sung, e.g.:

*You have put on Christ,
in him you have been baptised.
Alleluia, Alleluia.*

LORD'S PRAYER

The Celebrant stands in front of the altar and addresses the people:

CELEBRANT: Dearly beloved, this child has (these children have) been reborn in baptism. He/she (They) are now called children of God, for so indeed they are. In Confirmation he/she (they) receive the fullness of God's Spirit. In holy communion he/she (they) will share the banquet of Christ's sacrifice, calling God their Father in the midst of the Church. In their name, in the Spirit of our common sonship, let us pray together in the words that our Lord has given us.

ALL: Our Father . . .

BLESSING

The Celebrant blesses the mothers, who hold their children in their arms.

CELEBRANT: God the Father, through his Son, the Virgin Mary's child, has brought joy to all Christian mothers, as they see hope of eternal life shine on their children. May he bless the mother(s) of this child (these children). She (they) now thanks God for the gift of her child. May she/they be one with him/her in thanking him for ever in heaven, in Christ Jesus our Lord.

ALL: Amen.

The Celebrant blesses the fathers, and afterwards the entire assembly:

God is the giver of all life, human and divine. May he bless the father(s) of this child (these children). With his wife he will be the first teacher of his child in the ways of faith. May he be also the best of teachers, bearing witness to the faith by what he says and does, in Christ Jesus our Lord.

ALL: Amen.

CELEBRANT: By God's gift through water and the Holy Spirit we are reborn to everlasting life. In his goodness, may he continue to pour out his blessings upon all present who are his sons and daughters. May he make them always, wherever they may be, faithful members of his holy People. May he send his peace upon all who are gathered here, in Christ Jesus our Lord.

ALL: Amen.

CELEBRANT: May Almighty God the Father, and the Son, and the Holy Spirit, bless you.

ALL: Amen.

After the blessing all may sing an appropriate hymn expressing thanksgiving and paschal joy.

Confirmation

Confirmation is not just something that happened to you some time ago and can now be forgotten. In Confirmation the Holy Spirit came to you and continues to stay in you in a most special way. When you were confirmed you were given responsibility in the Church. You were officially commissioned to do the work of Jesus himself – to help to bring all men to the knowledge, love and service of the Father. This is a man-sized job and greater than you could undertake on your own: that's why you were given (like St Peter and his friends on Whit Sunday,) the Holy Spirit to make you powerful for God, to face the difficulties of a christian life courageously.

The sponsor at confirmation is not only there to act as a witness of an important happening. By placing his right hand on the shoulder of the person to be confirmed, he shows that he will offer his support and encouragement for as long as it is needed.

The Ceremony usually starts with this hymn:

Come, Holy Ghost, creator, come
From thy bright heavenly throne,
Come take possession of our souls
And make them all thy own.

Thou who art called the Paraclete
Best gift of God above,

The living spring, the living fire,
Sweet unction and true love.

Thou who art sevenfold in thy grace,
Finger of God's right hand;
His promise teaching little ones
To speak and understand.

O guide our minds with thy blessed light
With love our hearts inflame,
And with thy strength which ne'er decays
Confirm our mortal frame.

Far from us drive our deadly foe;
True peace unto us bring,
And through all perils lead us safe
Beneath thy sacred wing.

Through thee may we the Father know,
Through thee the eternal Son,
And thee the Spirit of them both
Thrice-blessed three in One.

All glory to the Father be
With his coequal son!
The same to thee, great Paraclete,
While endless ages run. Amen.

THE BISHOP: May the Holy Spirit come down upon you,
and may the power of the most high God keep you
free from every sin.

ALL: Amen.

BISHOP: Our help is in the name of the Lord.

ALL: Who made heaven and earth.

BISHOP: Lord, hear my prayer.

ALL: And let my cry come unto thee.

BISHOP: The Lord be with you.

ALL: And also with you.

BISHOP: Almighty and everlasting God who has given new life through water and the Holy Spirit to these your servants, and granted them forgiveness of all their sins, send down upon them from heaven your Holy Spirit, the Paraclete, with his sevenfold gifts.

ALL: Amen.

BISHOP: The Spirit of Wisdom and Understanding.

ALL: Amen.

BISHOP: The Spirit of Council and of Fortitude.

ALL: Amen.

BISHOP: The Spirit of Knowledge and of Piety.

ALL: Amen.

BISHOP: Fill them with reverent fear of yourself and in your goodness mark them out for eternal life with the sign of the cross of Christ. Through the same Jesus Christ, your Son, our Lord, who lives with you in the unity of the same Holy Spirit, God for ever –

ALL: Amen.

Each person to be confirmed now goes up to the Bishop. His sponsor goes with him and gives the card (on which the confirmation name is written) to the priest at the Bishop's side. The Bishop holds the blessed oil (chrism) in a container. He dips his thumb into the chrism and having laid his hand on the head of the person to be confirmed then traces a cross on the forehead. From the time the Church began, the 'laying on of hands' has been the sign used to show that the Holy Spirit was given to a person. Oil has always been used to consecrate people for a special work:

Kings and Queens – *by Confirmation we are made Kings and Queens.*

In Christ's kingdom the Kings and Queens are the servants of all. So we are marked out for service.

Prophets – *A prophet is one who is a witness. By Confirmation we become witnesses of Jesus Christ.*

Priests — *We are made priests at Confirmation, able to share in the work of Jesus.*

BISHOP: I sign you with the sign of the Cross and I confirm you with the Chrism of Salvation, in the name of the Father and of the Son and of the Holy Spirit.

RESPONSE: Amen.

At one time the Bishop, to show how grateful he was for the help that a person offered in accepting Confirmation would give a sign of affection by an embrace. Now he touches the person lightly on the cheek for the same reason.

BISHOP: Peace be with you.

One of the assistant priests wipes the oil off his forehead and the person, now confirmed, returns to his place.
When all have been confirmed, the Bishop, having washed his hands says the following prayer:

O God, you gave your Holy Spirit to the apostles and you willed that through them and through those who should come after them, he should be given to the rest of the faithful, look favourably upon this humble fulfilment of our office, and grant that the same Spirit coming into the hearts of those whose foreheads we have marked with sacred chrism and signed with the sign of the holy cross, may dwell therein and make of them living temples of his glory who livest and reignest with the Father and same Holy Spirit, God for ever and ever.

ALL: Amen.

BISHOP: Thus shall every man be blessed who fears the Lord. May the Lord of heaven bless you from Sion and all the days of your earthly life keep before your eyes the treasures of the heavenly Jerusalem. And may eternal life be yours.

ALL: Amen.

Confession

The Sacrament of Reconciliation

When we go to Confession we meet Jesus who takes us to himself and, because we are in him and because we are sorry, God our Father forgives us.

Each time we sin, we damage the loving relationship that exists between God our Father and ourselves, between Jesus our Brother and ourselves, between the Holy Spirit and ourselves, and between ourselves and the Church. If we sin very seriously, we cannot expect that just to mutter a few whispered words and listen to the priest say the absolution, is going automatically to make things right. There has to be a real change of heart in us. We must be determined with God's help to alter what is wrong. We go to confession not so much to 'get rid of sins' but to renew our friendship with God, to be strengthened and receive help. Each time we sin even though the sin may be an entirely private affair we harm the other members of God's family. We are all members of Christ's Body, the Church. A sin hurts us individually and so affects all other members. St Paul writes: 'If one part is hurt, all parts are hurt with it'.* That is why it is not just enough to apologise to God, we must also apologise to God's people, whose deputy is the priest. You will see (below) how the priest offers pardon to a person not

(*1 Corinthians 12, 26.)

only in the name of God but also in the name of the Church.

So when we go to confession although what we say to the priest and what he says to us is absolutely private, what we are doing is something public. It is much more than when in the privacy of our bedrooms, during our night prayers, we kneel down and tell God we are sorry.

It is for this reason that more and more frequently public services of sorrow are held in which people join together in preparing for the Sacrament of Reconciliation. One such service is given below. (See page 84.) However, it is likely that most people will still go to confession without that sort of communal preparation. Here then are some suggested prayers that might be used on the occasion of an individual celebration of this Sacrament.

For Individual Use

I may begin by asking the Holy Spirit, the Spirit of Jesus to help me to realise how I need God's pardon, that he will move me to be truly sorry, that he will help me to see myself as I really am and so search out my sins and failings.

This prayer would be best said in your own words. The following is only a suggestion:

O Spirit of Jesus be with me now.
I have sinned and I stand in need of pardon and help.
Lead me to true sorrow for my sins.
I ask you to help me to search my mind.
If you do not help me, I shall see only what I want to see. I shall make excuses for myself.
And so I ask you to help me to look at my daily living.
Let me see myself as I truly am.

I may next review my life since I last came to confession.
One way of doing this would be first to think about my
relationships with other people:

> *With those at home and also those who are related to me*
> *but who do not live under the same roof.*

Have I treated them with the dignity and respect they
deserve as well loved children of God? Have I
consistently tried to make them happy even at a cost
to my convenience? Or have I been selfish at home,
moody, inconsiderate of others' feelings, neither sharing things with them, nor working with them for the
good of all?

My relationship with my parents? grandparents?
My relationship with my children?
My relationship with my husband/wife?

With those at work:

Have I cooperated with them for the good of all?
Have I been honest with my employer/employees/
teachers – in the matter of time-keeping, work
materials, and quality of work?

With those I meet:

Have I been considerate towards other road-users?

Next I may think of the gifts God has given me. Have I
used them to the best of my ability? Have I used them
to make this world of his a better place?

The Gift of Health and Strength

Have I damaged it by over-eating, over-drinking, over-
smoking or lack of sleep?

The Gift of Intelligence

Have I hampered its use through spending too much
time watching or reading trash, or in day-dreaming,
or in futile conversations?

The Gift of Work

Have I tried to work honestly and well? Have I used at least part of my money for the relief of suffering in those less fortunate than myself?

The Gift of Sight

Have I used my eyes as God my Father would have wanted, to notice the needs of others, to enjoy and be amazed at all the good things around me? Or have I used my sight to photograph for my mind images that will later be used as sinful memories?

Has my sight led me to look critically at others, searching for the speck that is there while I ignore the planks of wood lodged in my own eyes?

The Gift of Hearing

Have I used my ability to hear as God my Father would have wished – to listen to other people, to listen to the suggestions my colleagues make, to listen to the requests my own family make of me? Am I a listening man or am I still immature and show it by boring other people with stories about myself?

The Gift of Speech

Have I used it as God my Father would have wished? To relate only the good I hear about people, and not the bad. To bring about harmony and unity between people, races, creeds. Or have I been harsh and critical in my speech, condemning others, relating gossip, blackening people's characters, unkind *to* people and unkind *about* people? Have I spoken the truth?

The Gift of Sex

Have I used (or not used) this gift as God my Father would have wished? Or have I betrayed his trust in

me by misusing this precious gift, using it before he
sanctions its use through the Sacrament of Marriage,
or using it selfishly simply for my own pleasure and
not as an expression of love towards my spouse?

The Gift of Leisure

Have I used my leisure time constructively? Have I
allowed my use of leisure to encroach on my family
dutires? Have I spent more on my leisure and com-
forts than I have offered in care for others and for the
support of my Parish?

Lastly I may think of my relationship with God my
Father, Jesus my Brother, the Holy Spirit. Have I
spoken with God as a real father, or have I ignored him,
or just gabbled a few prayers from time to time?

Have I been concerned for God's honour, wanting his
name known and loved by all? Have I had faith in the
realness of Jesus, close to me now? Have I trusted him
and realised that if I am not in him I am worth nothing?
Have I loved him and shown my love by 'keeping his
commandments' and showing the same love to others as
he showed to me?

Have I listened to the Holy Spirit? Have I tried to do
as he told me? Have I believed that I can do no good of
myself but only in the power the Holy Spirit gives me.

Now I try to express my sorrow in prayer. Again, the
words I make up myself are the best.

The following prayer is no more than an example:

O God my Father, I am truly sorry for having turned
away from your friendship. You have shown only love
towards me, and I have sometimes shown little love
in return.

For the sake of your Son, Jesus, who died and rose
again for me, forgive me all my sins.

I will try to make a fresh start with this confession. But I can do nothing unless your Holy Spirit helps me to lead a life such as Jesus led, a life spent forgetful of himself, in the service of others. (*See also page 24.*)

Now I am ready to go into the confessional. What I want to be able to do is to unburden myself to the priest. I do not need to think that I have to make a recitation of a list. Confession should be an opportunity for me to have a short chat with the priest. We all react to people differently and so it is helpful for a person, by trial, to find a priest who matches his temperament, and to whom he can speak easily.

Customs vary from place to place but the following formula might serve as a guide to the making of a confession. It is no more than a guide and could well be dispensed with altogether.

PENITENT: Please bless me, Father.

PRIEST: May our Lord Jesus bless you and help you to tell your sins.

PENITENT: I came to confession (three) (weeks) (months) ago. (*One need give only a very approximate time.*) I am (a schoolboy) (a mother) (a single person). I am very sorry for all my sins, especially. . . . Those are all the sins I can remember.

The priest may now give some helpful advice. He will also suggest something that you might do as a penance. Then he will say the following prayers:

PRIEST: May almighty God have mercy on you, forgive you your sins and bring you to everlasting life.

PENITENT: Amen.

PRIEST: May the almighty and merciful Lord grant you

pardon, absolution and remission of your sins.

PENITENT: Amen.

PRIEST: May our Lord Jesus Christ absolve you, and I, by his authority absolve you from every bond of excommunication and interdict*, so far as I can, and you have need. Therefore I absolve you from your sins in the name of the Father and of the Son, and of the Holy Spirit.

PENITENT: Amen.

PRIEST: May the passion of our Lord Jesus Christ, the merits of the blessed Virgin Mary and of all the saints, whatever good you shall have done and whatever evil (suffering) you shall have endured be to you for the remission of sins, increase of grace and the reward of eternal life.

PENITENT: Amen.

After I have finished my confession, I thank God my Father for forgiving me, and I pray my penance (if it is a prayer).

Parts of Psalm 103 make a good concluding prayer:

Bless the Lord, my soul,
bless his holy name, all that is in me.
Bless the Lord, my soul,
and remember all his kindnesses:
in forgiving all your offences,
in curing all your diseases,
in redeeming your life from the pit,
in crowning you with love and tenderness,

* These are penalties for certain sins that may be imposed by the Church.

in filling your years with prosperity,
in renewing your youth like an eagle's. . . .

The Lord is tender and compassionate,
slow to anger, most loving . . .
He never treats us, never punishes us
as our guilt and our sins deserve.

No less than the height of heaven over earth
is the greatness of his love for those who
    fear him;
he takes our sins farther away
than the east is from the west.

As tenderly as a father treats his children,
so the Lord treats those who fear him;
he knows what we are made of,
he remembers we are dust.

Man lasts no longer than grass
no longer than a wild flower he lives,
one gust of wind and he is gone,
never to be seen there again;

yet God's love for those who fear him,
lasts from all eternity and for ever. . . .

Glory be to the Father and to the Son and to the
    Holy Spirit,
As it was in the beginning, is now, and for ever shall
    be, world without end. Amen.

Service of Sorrow

A service of sorrow celebrated by a group of people helps one to realise that sin is not simply a private affair between oneself and God. All sins in some way harm other people, who are part of Christ's Body, of which I, by my sins, am an unhealthy member.

A service of sorrow may lead one to a deeper awareness of sin. The expressed sorrow of other people, the hymns and prayers said together, the readings from Scripture, all may dispose a person for confession with more sincerity than if he prepares silently and privately.

There is no question of a service of sorrow taking the place of confession. It normally presumes that private confession will follow.

The priest who absolves from sin also takes part in the service for he too is a sinner who needs to ask God for pardon.

Opening Hymn

(Tune: Nobody knows the trouble I've seen)

STAND

Chorus: Hear us, O Lord, we're calling on you
Come to our aid and help us.
Hear us, O Lord, we're calling on you
Pity us, and help us through.

1. I'm roving and I've gone astray, O my God
I just can't hear your voice today,

O my God.
It's hard, so hard, just hanging on,
> O my God.
Don't leave me lost and all forlorn,
> O my God.

2. All bold and proud, that's how I felt,
   > O my God.
   I wouldn't look to you for help, O my God.
   Then snares and traps they closed on me,
   > O my God.
   Now you alone can set me free, O my God.

3. My peace of mind is lost through sin,
   > O my God.
   I've only shame and fear within, O my God.
   O hear my cry of deep distress, O my God.
   And widen my heart's narrowness, O my God.

4. I really want to change my life, O my God.
   Though each step seems like too much strife,
   > O my God.
   Afraid to start, I'll lose the fight, O my God.
   So help me Lord, with all your might,
   > O my God.

KNEEL

PRIEST: Let us pray:

O God our Father, your family on earth is burdened with sin; source of reconciliation and peace, open our minds to the gift of sorrow so that we may be gathered in oneness. We make this prayer to you through Jesus Christ our Lord.

PRIEST: Lord, have mercy.
ALL: Lord have mercy.

Continue as at Mass:

PRIEST: O God, our Father, we know our own weakness. Our minds are darkened and by ourselves we cannot see the truth: our wills are weak, and by ourselves we cannot resist temptation; our hearts are fickle and by ourselves we cannot walk your way. So this day we ask you to give us light to see where we have failed you.

FIRST READER: Like Daniel in the Old Testament we will turn to God and seek him by prayer. 'O Lord, the great and holy God, you keep covenant and steadfast love with those who love you; we have sinned and done wrong and acted wickedly and rebelled. To you, O Lord, belongs all holiness, but to us guilt and trouble. To you, Lord our God, belongs mercy and forgiveness – O Lord, hear; O Lord, forgive; O Lord, give heed and act; delay not, for your own sake, because we are your people and are called by your name' (*Daniel* 9).

Hymn

Bless us and show us your mercy,
and smile on your people, O Lord.
Let all the earth know your wisdom,
let every man worship your will.

Sing, all mankind, with rejoicing,
for he is the God of the just.
Justice he gives to his people,
with fairness he rules all the world.

Fruits of the earth and the harvest
are gifts from the hand of the Lord.
Bless us and show us your mercy,
Let every man worship your will.

Glory to God through the ages,
all honour and praise to your name:
Father and Son and the Spirit
let every man worship your will.

SIT

SECOND READER:

> *The reader gives a summary of the story of David's sin, so
> that the following reading will make sense:*

The Lord sent Nathan the prophet to
David. He came to him and said:
'In the same town were two men,
one rich, the other poor.
The rich man had flocks and herds
in great abundance;
the poor man had nothing but a ewe lamb,
one only, a small one he had bought.
This he fed, and it grew up with him and his children,
eating his bread, drinking from his cup,
sleeping on his breast; it was like a daughter to him.
When there came a traveller to stay, the rich man
refused to take one of his own flock or herd
to provide for the wayfarer who had come to him.
Instead he took the poor man's lamb
and prepared it for his guest.'
David's anger flared up. 'As the Lord lives,' he said
to Nathan 'the man who did this deserves to die! He
must make fourfold restitution for the lamb, for doing
such a thing and showing no compassion.'
Then Nathan said to David, 'You are the man.'
(*2 Samuel 12, 1–7.*)

First Examination of Conscience
KNEEL

PRIEST: Have we not been more concerned for our own rights than for God's glory?

ALL: Have mercy on us Lord, *we* are the ones who have sinned.

This prayer is repeated after each question.

– Have we not been more concerned about the little things that disturb us than the injustices in the world?

– Our prayers have been more a lip-service said out of duty than a loving conversation between children and their loving Father.

– We have been kind to those who have been kind to us, but have we not neglected those who appeared to be indifferent to us?

– Often we have brought our gift to the altar without first being reconciled with our brother.

– More often we are content to do the least possible amount of work instead of doing our best and using the energy you have given us.

– Have we not treated other people as things, instead of with the respect that we owe to them as human persons?

– Do we look to the Eucharist as a duty to be got through or a privilege to partake of?

– Do we take seriously the duty we have to deepen our faith by reading and discussion?

– How ready we are to spend our money on ourselves, and how slow to seek ways and means of using it for others.

Short pause for reflection.

SIT

THIRD READER:

Introduce as the gospel at Mass.

After the resurrection Jesus revealed himself again to the disciples by the Sea of Tiberias.

'After the meal Jesus said to Simon Peter, "Simon son of John, do you love me more than these others do?" He answered, "Yes Lord, you know I love you". Jesus said to him, "Feed my lambs". A second time he said to him, "Simon son of John, do you love me?" He replied, "Yes, Lord, you know I love you". Jesus said to him, "Look after my sheep". Then he said to him a third time, "Simon son of John, do you love me?" Peter was upset that he asked him for the third time "Do you love me?" and said, "Lord, you know everything; you know I love you". Jesus said to him, "Feed my sheep." ' (*John 21, 15–17*)

Second Examination of Conscience

KNEEL

PRIEST: We more often seek only our own ease and comfort and forget your wish, Lord, that your followers should take up their cross every day and follow you.

ALL: We have sinned, but you know that we want to love you.

This prayer is repeated after every question.

– How reluctant we are to apologise for having offended another and how quick to turn on those who offend us.

– We are often conceited in our opinions and unwilling to listen to the advice others may offer.

– How little trust we have that you will care for our future, Lord; we spend our time worrying about ourselves and our concerns.

– Often we are quick-tempered, impatient and intolerant

when things do not go as we want them to.
- Do we not criticise other people for doing things we allow ourselves to do?
- Have we not been very blind to other people's troubles when we should have identified ourselves with them?
- God in his love has given us many gifts – have we used them for the benefit of others?
- Maybe we have sometimes let our fears of what others will think keep us from honouring God.
- My person is sacred. Have I treated my body with disrespect or allowed others to do so. Have I neglected myself by lack of sleep and food?

Short pause for reflection.

PRIEST: Let us pray.

ALL: We are not only guilty towards God, our merciful and kindly Father in heaven, and to Our Lord Jesus Christ who has suffered for us. We are also guilty to our brothers and sisters, the whole community of God's people. Through our sins, love grows cold in the Body of Christ, the Church. We will confess our guilt before God and before one another.
I confess (and to you, brethren).

PRIEST: May the Lord be in your heart and on your lips that you may humbly confess your sins before God, and His Saints and before His Church, in the name of the Father and of the Son and of the Holy Spirit.

Individual confessions may follow if desired.

The Lord is my good shepherd   (*Psalm 23*)
he cares for all my needs.
He gives me rest in meadows
where grass is green and fresh,

He is the best of shepherds,
his path is sure and safe.
He leads me where the waters
refresh my weary soul.

I will not fear the darkness
for you are at my side.
Your arm is there to lean on,
your gentle strength is mine.

You let me feast in safety
while all my foes looked on,
You gave me rank and honour,
I could not wish for more.

Your kindness will not leave me
as long as life shall last.
I live for ever, sharing
God's holy house with him.

All praise to God the Father,
all glory to the Son;
and to the Holy Spirit
a hymn of endless praise.

O God, our Father, direct and control us in every part
of our life. Control our tongues that we may speak no
false, angry, or impure words. Control our actions that
we may do nothing to shame ourselves or hurt others.
Control our minds that we may think no evil, bitter, or
irreverent thoughts. Control our hearts that they may
be set only on pleasing you. Through Our Lord Jesus
Christ, Amen.

The Mass

The Mass is a mystery. That does not mean to say that we cannot understand it. It means this: that although every year we will grow to appreciate its meaning more and more, we will never be able to say, 'Now I understand everything there is to know about the Mass'.

Nor will anyone ever be able to write a complete explanation of the Mass. The few lines that follow, and the introductions to each of the four Eucharistic prayers, are merely a few thoughts which the reader may find helpful.

A Very Special Meal

In March every year Jewish families had a special meal which they looked forward to rather as we look forward to our Christmas dinner. As a young boy, Jesus would be excited on the Paschal eve because he, like every boy in a Jewish family, had a special part to play. After the table had been prepared and special dishes laid upon it, he had to ask Joseph this question: 'How is this night different from all other nights? For on all other nights we may eat either leavened or unleavened bread, but on this night only unleavened. On all other nights we may eat other kinds of herb, but on this night only bitter herbs. . . . On all other nights we eat either sitting upright or reclining, but on this night we all recline. . . .' And

Joseph, like the Heads of all the other families in the land, would describe how this meal was very special indeed.

A New Life in a New Land

The meal recalled the two main events in the history of the Jews: their deliverance by God from the slavery in Egypt and the agreement made by God with Moses as the representative of the people. This agreement was called the 'Covenant'. The people agreed at Mount Sinai in the desert, to keep God's Commandments: 'All that the Lord has said that we will do', they shouted together. Then Moses built an altar and he poured part of the blood of an animal sacrifice over the altar (which represented God) and sprinkled the rest over the people. The Jews thought of blood as the very life of a person. So in this ceremony Moses is making it clear that God was henceforth willing to share his life with them. Moses ended the ceremony by saying these words 'This is the blood of the Covenant that God has made with you'.

Every year, the Jews at this Paschal meal not only thanked God for saving them and renewed their Covenant with him, they relived this experience of the past and joined themselves to Moses and his people on this march to a new life in a new land.

During Supper

The last meal Jesus had with his apostles before he died was this Paschal meal. But a Paschal meal in which this ancient ceremony was changed greatly. Perhaps the meal began in the normal way with John, the youngest present, putting the traditional

questions to Jesus as the 'father' of the family. But
then, later, as Jesus took the bread and broke it, he
told them that this was his body which would be
sacrificed for them. And as he passed the cup to them
he said 'This is my blood, the blood of the Covenant
which is to be poured out for many for the forgiveness of sins'.(Matthew 26, 27.) The apostles would immediately remember the words Moses had said when he
and his followers ratified the agreement made between
God and themselves. They would see that Jesus was
making a new Covenant with His Father.

In all the houses of Jerusalem the people were
taking part in a Paschal meal 'in memory of Moses'.
Jesus said 'Do this in memory of me'. In all the
other Paschal meals the people were expressing their
willingness to abide by the ten Commandments. But
Jesus went further, 'I give you a new commandment:
love one another; just as I have loved you, you
must love one another.' (John 15, 12.) Later on he
repeated the same commandment: 'This is my
commandment; love one another as I have loved
you.' (John 15, 17).

What we do at Mass

This then is what we do at Mass. We not only thank
God for sending Jesus to save us from slavery to sin,
we give ourselves to the Father, with Jesus. We say
'This is my body and my blood – my whole life
offered with the sacrifice Jesus made of His whole
life to the Father'. We especially make the Sunday
Mass an expression of the way we have tried to live
in friendship with others during the week. If I am
hurting others in any way, or keeping people apart,

then my partaking of this meal is a mockery, a pretence. You remember Jesus' words, 'If your brother has anything against you, leave your gift on the altar and first go and be reconciled.' (Matthew 5, 24.)

It's a Celebration

Yes, that's what we call the Mass – a celebration. What is celebration? A happy event, usually accompanying a meal, shared by friends. This is what the Mass should be – not just the dreary and routine fulfilment of a Church law, but a happy happening, a real celebration looking forward to that day of supreme celebration, when at journey's end, God's people are united in the never-ending family reunion of Heaven.

The Order of Mass

Prayers of Greeting

HYMN during the Entrance.

STAND

PRIEST: In the name of the Father, and of the Son, and of the Holy Spirit.

ALL: Amen.

PRIEST: The Lord be with you.

ALL: And also with you.

Alternative greeting

PRIEST: The grace of our Lord Jesus Christ and the love of God and the fellowship of the Holy Spirit be with you all.

ALL: And also with you.

or

PRIEST: The grace and peace of God our Father and the Lord Jesus Christ be with you.

ALL: Blessed be God, the Father of our Lord Jesus Christ.
   or And also with you.

Prayers of Sorrow

PRIEST: My brothers and sisters, to prepare ourselves to

celebrate the sacred mysteries, let us call to mind our sins. (*Pause.*)

ALL: I confess to almighty God,
and to you, my brothers and sisters,
that I have sinned through my own fault, (strike breast once) in my thoughts and in my words,
in what I have done,
and in what I have failed to do;
and I ask blessed Mary, ever virgin,
all the angels and saints,
and you, my brothers and sisters
to pray for me to the Lord our God.

Alternative prayers of sorrow

PRIEST: My brothers and sisters, to prepare ourselves to celebrate the sacred mysteries, let us call to mind our sins. (*Pause.*)
Lord, we have sinned against you:
Lord, have mercy.

ALL: Lord, have mercy.

PRIEST: Lord, show us your mercy and love.

ALL: And grant us your salvation.

or

PRIEST: My brothers and sisters, to prepare ourselves to celebrate the sacred mysteries, let us call to mind our sins. (*Pause.*)

PRIEST: You were sent to heal the contrite:
Lord, have mercy.

ALL: Lord, have mercy.

PRIEST: You came to call sinners:
Christ, have mercy.

ALL: Christ, have mercy.

R—CPB—D

PRIEST: You plead for us at the right hand of the Father:
Lord, have mercy.

ALL: Lord, have mercy.

The absolution

PRIEST: May almighty God have mercy on us,
forgive us our sins,
and bring us to everlasting life.

ALL: Amen.

PRIEST: Lord, have mercy

ALL: Lord, have mercy.

PRIEST: Christ, have mercy.

ALL: Christ, have mercy.

PRIEST: Lord, have mercy.

ALL: Lord, have mercy.

PRIEST: Glory be to God on high,

ALL (*Priest and People together*): And on earth peace to
men who are God's friends. We praise thee. We bless
thee. We adore thee. We glorify thee. We give thee
thanks for thy great glory. Lord God, heavenly king,
God the almighty Father. Lord Jesus Christ, only
begotten Son. Lord God, Lamb of God, Son of the
Father.

Thou who takest away the sins of the world, have
mercy on us. Thou who takest away the sins of the
world, receive our prayer.

Thou who art seated at the right hand of the Father,
have mercy on us. For thou alone art the Holy One.
Thou alone art the Lord. Thou alone art the Most
High, Jesus Christ.

With the Holy Spirit;
In the glory of God the Father. Amen.

PRIEST: Let us pray.

There is a moment's pause for all to pray silently. Then the priest says the prayer of the day. At the end –

ALL: Amen.

Liturgy of the Word

SIT

There are usually three readings. The first one may be from the Old Testament – that is, one of the scripture writings compiled before our Lord was born. The second one will be from one of the New Testament writings, excluding the Gospels. The reader ends each reading with:

This is the Word of the Lord

ALL: Thanks be to God.

Verses from a psalm may be said or sung after each reading. The final reading is taken from one of the four Gospels.

STAND

PRIEST: The Lord be with you.

ALL: And also with you.

PRIEST: A reading from the holy gospel according to—

ALL: Glory to you, Lord.

At the end of the Gospel –

PRIEST: This is the gospel of the Lord.

ALL: Praise to you, Lord Jesus Christ.

SIT

The priest may now give a talk. We sit and listen. We respond by expressing our belief in God's word.

STAND

PRIEST: I believe in one God.

ALL: The almighty Father, maker of heaven and earth, maker of all things, visible and invisible.

I believe in one Lord, Jesus Christ, the only begotten Son of God, born of the Father before time began. God from God, Light from Light, true God from true God; begotten not made, one in substance with the Father; and through him all things were made.

For us men and for our salvation he came down from heaven (*all bow*), was incarnate of the Virgin Mary by the power of the Holy Spirit, and was made man.

For our sake too, under Pontius Pilate, he was crucified, suffered death and was buried.

The third day he rose from the dead, as the scriptures had foretold.

He ascended into heaven, where he is seated at the right hand of the Father. He will come again in glory to judge the living and the dead, and his kingdom will have no end.

I believe in the Holy Spirit, the Lord, the giver of life, who proceeds from the Father and the Son. Together with the Father and the Son he is adored and glorified; he it was who spoke through the prophets.

I believe in one, holy, catholic, and apostolic Church. I profess one baptism for the remission of sins. And I look forward to the resurrection of the dead, and the life of the world to come. Amen.

The priest now invites the people to pray with him for the needs of the world, the Church, and the local community.

Liturgy of the Eucharist
THE OFFERING OF BREAD AND WINE
SIT

PRIEST: Blessed are you, Lord, God of all creation.
Through your goodness we have this bread to offer,
which earth has given and human hands have made.
It will become for us the bread of life.

ALL: Blessed be God for ever.

PRIEST: By the mystery of this water and wine
may we come to share in the divinity of Christ,
who humbled himself to share in our humanity.

Blessed are you, Lord, God of all creation.
Through your goodness we have this wine to offer,
fruit of the vine and work of human hands.
It will become our spiritual drink.

ALL: Blessed be God for ever.

PRIEST: Lord God, we ask you to receive us
and be pleased with the sacrifice we offer you
with humble and contrite hearts.
As the priest washes his hands, he says:
Lord, wash away my iniquity;
cleanse me from my sin.

STAND

PRIEST: Pray, brethren, that our sacrifice
may be acceptable to God, the almighty Father.

ALL: May the Lord accept the sacrifice at your hands,
for the praise and glory of his name,
for our good, and the good of all his Church.

*The priest now says a prayer over the offerings to which
all answer: Amen.*

THE EUCHARISTIC PRAYER

PRIEST: The Lord be with you.

ALL: And also with you.

PRIEST: Let us lift up our hearts.

ALL: We have raised them up to the Lord.

PRIEST: Let us give thanks to the Lord our God.

ALL: It is right and fitting.

> *The priest now says a prayer (called the preface). At the end:*

ALL: Holy, holy, holy, Lord God of hosts.
Thy glory fills all heaven and earth. Hosanna in the highest. Blessed is he who comes in the name of the Lord. Hosanna in the highest.

KNEEL

> *One of the Eucharistic Prayers is now said. These are given on pages 107, 111, 114 and 118.*

> *The conclusion of each prayer is as follows:*

PRIEST: Through him,
with him,
in him,
in the unity of the Holy Spirit,
all glory and honour is yours,
almighty Father,
for ever and ever.

ALL: Amen.

The Rite of Communion

PRIEST: Let us pray with confidence to the Father in the words our Saviour gave us:

ALL (*Priest and people together*): Our Father, who art in heaven,

hallowed be thy name,
thy kingdom come,
thy will be done on earth as it is in heaven.
Give us this day our daily bread,
and forgive us our trespasses,
as we forgive those who trespass against us,
and lead us not into temptation,
but deliver us from evil.

PRIEST: Deliver us, Lord, from every evil,
and grant us peace in our day.
In your mercy keep us free from sin
and protect us from all anxiety
as we wait in joyful hope
for the coming of our Saviour, Jesus Christ.

ALL: For the kingdom, the power and the glory are yours
now and for ever.

PRIEST: Lord Jesus Christ, you said to your apostles:
I leave you peace, my peace I give you.
Look not on our sins, but on the faith of your Church,
and grant us the peace and unity of your kingdom
where you live for ever and ever.

ALL: Amen.

PRIEST: The peace of the Lord be with you always.

ALL: And also with you.

The priest may then say: 'Let us offer each other the sign of peace'. A gesture of peace may be made from one to another. Meanwhile the priest breaks the host.

PRIEST: May this mingling of the body and blood of our
Lord Jesus Christ bring eternal life to us who receive it.

ALL: Lamb of God, you take away the sins of the world:
have mercy on us.
Lamb of God, you take away the sins of the world:
have mercy on us.

Lamb of God, you take away the sins of the world:
   grant us peace.

KNEEL

PRIEST: Lord Jesus Christ, Son of the living God,
   by the will of the Father and the work of the Holy
      Spirit,
   your death brought life to the world.
   By your holy body and blood
   free me from all my sins and from every evil.
   Keep me faithful to your teaching,
   and never let me be parted from you.

   or

Lord Jesus Christ,
with faith in your love and mercy,
I eat your body and drink your blood.
Let it not bring me condemnation,
but health in mind and body.

This is the Lamb of God
who takes away the sins of the world.
Happy are those who are called to his supper.

ALL: Lord, I am not worthy to receive you,
   but only say the word and I shall be healed.

   *While the priest himself receives Communion, verses from
   the psalms are said or sung. As the priest gives Communion
   to the people, each replies, Amen.*

SIT

   *After Communion there may be a period of silence for
   private prayer. (See page 130.) Then the priest says the
   final prayer to which all respond Amen.*

STAND

PRIEST: The Lord be with you.

ALL: And also with you.

PRIEST: May almighty God bless you, the Father, and the Son, and the Holy Spirit.

ALL: Amen.

PRIEST: The Mass is ended, go in peace.

ALL: Thanks be to God.

or

PRIEST: Go in the peace of Christ,
  or Go in peace to love and serve the Lord.

ALL: Thanks be to God.

The Four
Eucharistic Prayers

Some people have been helped to understand the order of the Mass by remembering that during the Mass

> *WE SPEAK TO GOD*
> *GOD SPEAKS TO US*
> *WE GIVE TO GOD*
> *GOD GIVES TO US*

So far in the Mass, we have spoken to God (in the introductory prayers, pages 96 to 99), God has spoken to us (in the Liturgy of the word, page 99), we have given to God (at the offering of bread and wine, page 101), and Jesus now is going to transform our gifts of bread and wine into himself. In each of these four prayers you will read and you will hear the priest say the very words Jesus used at the Last Supper when he changed the bread and wine of the Paschal meal into himself – and then told his friends to do what he had done, and gave them the power to do so. At this point in the Mass we offer ourselves with Jesus Christ to his Father. The Father shows that he accepts our offering, our sacrifice, by inviting us to share the gift with him. God gives his own well-loved Son to us in Communion. That is why one should always try to receive Communion at every Mass.

Eucharistic Prayer 1.

KNEEL

We come to you, Father,
with praise and thanksgiving,
through Jesus Christ your Son.
Through him we ask you to accept and bless
these gifts we offer you in sacrifice.
We offer them for your holy catholic Church,
watch over it, Lord, and guide it;
grant it peace and unity throughout the world.
We offer them for *N. . .* our Pope,
for *N. . .* our bishop,
and for all who hold and teach the catholic faith
that comes to us from the apostles.

Remember, Lord, your people,
especially those for whom we now pray, *N.* and *N.*
    (Pause.)
Remember all of us gathered here before you.
You know how firmly we believe in you
and dedicate ourselves to you.
We offer you this sacrifice of praise
for ourselves and those who are dear to us.
We pray to you, our living and true God,
for our well-being and redemption.

In union with the whole Church
we honour Mary,
the ever-virgin mother of Jesus Christ, our Lord and
    God.
We honour Joseph, her husband,
the apostles and martyrs
Peter and Paul, Andrew
   the following words in brackets may be omitted.

(James, John, Thomas,
James, Philip,
Bartholomew, Matthew, Simon and Jude;
we honour Linus, Cletus, Clement, Sixtus,
Cornelius, Cyprian, Lawrence, Chrysogonus,
John and Paul, Cosmas and Damian)
and all the saints.
May their merits and prayers
gain us your constant help and protection.
(Through Christ our Lord. Amen.)

Father, accept this offering
from your whole family.
Grant us your peace in this life,
save us from final damnation,
and count us among those you have chosen.

Bless and approve our offering;
make it acceptable to you,
an offering in spirit and in truth.
Let it become for us
the body and blood of Jesus Christ,
your only Son, our Lord.

The day before he suffered
he took bread in his sacred hands
and looking up to heaven,
to you, his almighty Father,
he gave you thanks and praise.
He broke the bread,
gave it to his disciples, and said:
Take this, all of you, and eat it:
this is my body which will be given up for you.

When supper was ended,
he took the cup.
Again he gave you thanks and praise,

gave the cup to his disciples, and said:
Take this, all of you, and drink from it:
this is the cup of my blood,
the blood of the new and everlasting covenant.
It will be shed for you and for all men
so that sins may be forgiven.
Do this in memory of me.

Let us proclaim the mystery of faith:

ALL: Christ has died,
    Christ is risen,
    Christ will come again.

Alternatives

2. Dying you destroyed our death,
   rising you restored our life.
   Lord Jesus, come in glory.

3. When we eat this bread and drink this cup,
   we proclaim your death, Lord Jesus,
   until you come in glory.

4. Lord, by your cross and resurrection
   you have set us free.
   You are the Saviour of the world.

Father, we celebrate the memory of Christ, your Son.
We, your people and your ministers,
recall his passion,
his resurrection from the dead,
and his ascension into glory;
and from the many gifts you have given us
we offer to you, God of glory and majesty,
this holy and perfect sacrifice:
the bread of life
and the cup of eternal salvation.

Look with favour on these offerings

and accept them as once you accepted
the gifts of your servant Abel,
the sacrifice of Abraham, our father in faith,
and the bread and wine offered by your priest
    Melchisedech.

Almighty God,
we pray that your angel may take this sacrifice
to your altar in heaven.
Then, as we receive from this altar
the sacred body and blood of your Son,
let us be filled with every grace and blessing.
(Through Christ our Lord. Amen.)

Remember, Lord, those who have died
and have gone before us marked with the sign of faith,
especially those for whom we now pray *N.* and *N.* (*Pause.*)
May these, and all who sleep in Christ,
find in your presence
light, happiness, and peace.
(Through Christ our Lord. Amen.)

For ourselves, too, we ask
some share in the fellowship of your apostles and martyrs,
with John the Baptist, Stephen, Matthias, Barnabas,
(Ignatius, Alexander, Marcellinus, Peter,
Felicity, Perpetua, Agatha, Lucy,
Agnes, Cecilia, Anastasia)
and all the saints.
Though we are sinners,
we trust in your mercy and love.
Do not consider what we truly deserve,
but grant us your forgiveness.

Through Christ our Lord
you give us all these gifts.
You fill them with life and goodness.
You bless them and make them holy.

[*Turn now to
page 102.*]

Eucharistic Prayer 2

THE GREAT 'YES'

When Jesus walked the roads of Palestine, he was open both to God, his Father, and to the needs of all the people he met. This openness reached its climax in his death and resurrection. The Mass makes present this great 'yes' of Jesus' whole life.

If I wish to be close to Jesus Christ by faith I must, to some extent, share his outlook; I must have something of that same openness. I must be prepared to say 'Yes' to God, my Father, despite the difficulties. Like Jesus, I must try to say 'yes' to the needs of people and the demands they make of me.

The word 'Amen' means a very strong 'Yes'. This word is used frequently during the Mass. The 'great Amen' is the one that comes after the prayer: 'Through him (Jesus our Lord), with him, in him, in the unity of the Holy Spirit, all glory and honour is yours, almighty Father, for ever and ever. AMEN.' From the earliest times Christians have proclaimed a loud 'Amen' to this prayer.

Another important 'Amen' is the one I say just before Communion after the priest has said to me 'The Body of Christ'. This 'Amen' can mean for me: 'Yes, Lord. I believe this is you. I will try and live like you today: open to whatever your Father wants me to do, open to the needs of all the people I meet.'

Father, it is our duty and our salvation,
always and everywhere
to give you thanks
through your beloved Son, Jesus Christ.
He is the Word through whom you made the universe,

the Saviour you sent to redeem us.
By the power of the Holy Spirit
he took flesh and was born of the Virgin Mary.
For our sake he opened his arms on the cross;
he put an end to death
and revealed the resurrection.
In this he fulfilled your will
and won for you a holy people.
And so we join the angels and the saints
in proclaiming your glory
as we sing (say):
Holy, holy, holy Lord . . .

Lord, you are holy indeed,
the fountain of all holiness.
Let your Spirit come upon these gifts to make them holy,
so that they may become for us
the body and blood of our Lord, Jesus Christ.

Before he was given up to death,
a death he freely accepted,
he took bread and gave you thanks.
He broke the bread,
gave it to his disciples, and said:
Take this, all of you, and eat it:
this is my body which will be given up for you.

When supper was ended, he took the cup.
Again he gave you thanks and praise,
gave the cup to his disciples, and said:
Take this, all of you, and drink from it:
this is the cup of my blood,
the blood of the new and everlasting covenant.
It will be shed for you and for all men
so that sins may be forgiven.

Do this in memory of me.

Let us proclaim the mystery of faith:

ALL: Christ has died,
Christ is risen,
Christ will come again.

Alternatives

2. Dying you destroyed our death,
rising you restored our life.
Lord Jesus, come in glory.

3. When we eat this bread and drink this cup,
we proclaim your death, Lord Jesus,
until you come in glory.

4. Lord, by your cross and resurrection
you have set us free.
You are the Saviour of the world.

In memory of his death and resurrection,
we offer you, Father, this life-giving bread,
this saving cup.
We thank you for counting us worthy
to stand in your presence and serve you.
May all of us who share in the body and blood of Christ
be brought together in unity by the Holy Spirit.

Lord, remember your Church throughout the world;
make us grow in love,
together with *N.* . . our Pope,
N. . . our bishop, and all the clergy.*

Remember our brothers and sisters
who have gone to their rest

*In Mass for a dead person: Remember *N.* . . whom you
have called from this life.
In baptism he (she) died with Christ:
may he (she) also share his resurrection.

in the hope of rising again;
bring them and all the departed
into the light of your presence.
Have mercy on us all;
make us worthy to share eternal life
with Mary, the virgin mother of God,
with the apostles,
and with all the saints who have done your will throughout the ages.
May we praise you in union with them
and give you glory
through your Son, Jesus Christ.

Turn now to page 102.

Eucharistic Prayer 3

AROUND GOD'S TABLE

*There are all sorts of meals: meals to celebrate
jubilees; meals at weddings and meals at christenings;
there are welcome-home meals and farewell meals.*

*The Mass is a meal but a meal of a most special
sort: a sacrificial meal. This sacrificial meal was first
eaten by Jesus and his apostles the night before he
died. It was as if Jesus said to his friends: 'At this
farewell meal I am going to give you my very life.'
This, in fact, is what he meant when, as he took the
loaf, he said: 'This is my body which will be given up
for you', and as he took the cup, 'This is the cup of
my blood . . . It will be shed for you and for all men.'*

*We know that by these words which he utters
today through his priest at Mass, Jesus is totally and
truly giving himself for us. And so at Mass we are
taking part in a meal with Jesus Christ who gave
his life in sacrifice. By eating of this sacrifice we
pledge that we join ourselves to him.*

A family is united by the meal it shares. When we are at Mass, we are not simply a collection of individuals. We are God's family, brothers and sisters together around his table. This sacrificial meal unites us all. At some Masses this unity is expressed by the 'kiss of peace' ceremony. We would be hypocrites if we took part in the Mass with hatred in our hearts, or unwillingness to forgive, or with indifference to the needs of others, or even hard feelings towards those who annoy us.

'Father hear the prayers of the family you have gathered together here before you. In mercy and love unite all your children wherever they may be.'

Father, you are holy indeed
and all creation rightly gives you praise.
All life, all holiness comes from you
through your Son, Jesus Christ our Lord,
by the working of the Holy Spirit.

From age to age you gather a people to yourself,
so that from east to west
a perfect offering may be made
to the glory of your name.

And so, Father, we bring you these gifts.
We ask you to make them holy by the power of your
      Spirit,
that they may become for us the body and blood
of your Son, our Lord Jesus Christ,
at whose command we celebrate this eucharist.

On the night he was betrayed,
he took bread and gave you thanks and praise.
He broke the bread, gave it to his disciples, and said:
Take this, all of you, and eat it:
This is my body which will be given up for you.

When supper was ended, he took the cup.
Again he gave you thanks and praise,
gave the cup to his disciples, and said:
Take this, all of you, and drink from it:
this is the cup of my blood,
the blood of the new and everlasting covenant.
It will be shed for you and for all men
so that sins may be forgiven.
Do this in memory of me.

Let us proclaim the mystery of faith:

ALL: Christ has died,
Christ is risen,
Christ will come again.

Alternatives

2. Dying you destroyed our death,
rising you restored our life.
Lord Jesus, come in glory.

3. When we eat this bread and drink this cup,
we proclaim your death, Lord Jesus,
until you come in glory.

4. Lord, by your cross and resurrection
you have set us free.
You are the Saviour of the world.

Father, calling to mind the death your Son endured for
our salvation,
his glorious resurrection and ascension into heaven,
and ready to greet him when he comes again,
we offer you in thanksgiving this holy and living sacrifice.

Look with favour on your Church's offering,
and see the Victim whose death has reconciled us to
yourself.

Grant that we, who are nourished by his body and blood,
may be filled with his Holy Spirit,
and become one body, one spirit in Christ.

May he make us an everlasting gift to you
and enable us to share in the inheritance of your saints,
with Mary, the virgin mother of God;
with the apostles, the martyrs,
(Saint N. . . – patron saint or saint of the day), and all
    your saints,
on whose constant intercession we rely for help.

Lord may this sacrifice, which has made our peace with
    you,
advance the peace and salvation of all the world.
Strengthen in faith and love your pilgrim Church on
    earth:
your servant, Pope N. . . , our bishop N. . . ,
    and all the bishops,
with the clergy and the entire people your Son has
    gained for you.
Father, hear the prayers of the family you have gathered
    here before you.
In mercy and love unite all your children
wherever they may be.*

*In Mass for a dead person: Remember N. . . .
In Baptism he (she) died with Christ:
may he (she) also share his resurrection
when Christ will raise our mortal bodies
and make them like his own in glory.
Welcome into your kingdom our departed brothers and sisters,
and all who have left this world in your friendship.
There we hope to share in your glory
Father, we acknowledge your greatness:
all your actions show your wisdom and love.
We shall become like you
and praise you for ever through Christ our Lord,
from whom all good things come.

Welcome into your kingdom our departed brothers and
    sisters,
and all who have left this world in your friendship.
We hope to enjoy for ever the vision of your glory,
through Christ our Lord, from whom all good things
    come.
Turn now to page 102.

Eucharistic Prayer 4

GOD'S GREAT PLAN

God's great plan for men is like a four-act drama.

*The First Act lasted some two thousand years.
During that time God gradually prepared men for
the coming of his Son. He began by calling Abraham
to faith in himself. Through Abraham, God started
off a family. Many years later God made this family
into a people by choosing Moses. It was Moses who
led the Hebrews out of slavery in Egypt towards the
promised land. When the people had settled there
God called David to be their king. David's successor,
Solomon, was more concerned for his own glory than
God's and as a result the people were again taken
into slavery, this time in Babylon. All that came back
from Babylon was a tiny remnant of a people.
Because of the sufferings they had endured, they
realised that they needed a Saviour, a Messiah, and
they prayed God to send one. God answered their
prayers by sending his dearly beloved Son.*

*The Second Act is the thirty or so years of Jesus'
life in Palestine: his birth, his work, his death,
resurrection and ascension. This period is called the
'New Testament' or 'New Covenant'. Jesus replaced
the alliance (or 'testament' or 'covenant' – the words
mean the same thing) that God had made with men*

*in Act 1. Jesus' coming is the very summit of history;
there can never be a greater event than this.*

*In the Third Act Jesus continues the work he began
in Palestine. After his ascension nearly two thousand years ago, he sent his Spirit into the world so
that his work would go on. Preaching, teaching,
helping people in need – all this he continues through
his followers united together in his Church and filled
with his Spirit.*

*We are all in this plan of God's. We are made
part of it, 'inserted' into it by Baptism. Of course we
can opt out if we want. We are free to say Yes or
No. If No, then God's plan is halted – only for a
time. He can do without us. If Yes, then we are
helping this great plan forward towards its last
phase, the finale of the drama, when Jesus will come
in glory.*

*At Mass we think of these four Acts: we recall
the preparation in Act 1, we remember with gratitude
the coming of Jesus in Act 2. We who are in Act 3
renew at this Mass the consecration we accepted in
Baptism to work with God's continuing plan. At the
same time we look forward to the second coming of
Jesus, the 'Finale' of Act 4, when God's plan of our
salvation will be complete.*

Father in heaven, it is right that we should give you
  thanks and glory:
you alone are God, living and true.
Through all eternity you live in unapproachable light.
Source of life and goodness, you have created all things,
  to fill your creatures with every blessing
and lead all men to the joyful vision of your light.
Countless hosts of angels stand before you to do your will

they look upon your splendour
and praise you, night and day.
United with them, and in the name of every creature
    under heaven,
we too praise your glory as we sing (say):
Holy, holy, holy Lord . . .

Father, we acknowledge your greatness:
all your actions show your wisdom and love.
You formed man in your own likeness
and set him over the whole world
to serve you, his creator,
and to rule over all creatures.
Even when he disobeyed you and lost your friendship
you did not abandon him to the power of death,
but helped all men to seek and find you.
Again and again you offered a covenant to man,
and through the prophets taught him to hope for
    salvation.

Father, you so loved the world
that in the fullness of time you sent your only Son to
    be our Saviour.
He was conceived through the power of the Holy Spirit,
    and born of the Virgin Mary,
a man like us in all things but sin.
To the poor he proclaimed the good news of salvation,
to prisoners, freedom,
and to those in sorrow, joy.
In fulfilment of your will
he gave himself up to death;
but by rising from the dead,
he destroyed death and restored life.
And that we might live no longer for ourselves but for
    him,

he sent the Holy Spirit from you, Father,
as his first gift to those who believe,
to complete his work on earth
and bring us the fullness of grace.

Father, may this Holy Spirit sanctify these offerings.
Let them become the body and blood of Jesus Christ
  our Lord
as we celebrate the great mystery
which he left us as an everlasting covenant.

He always loved those who were his own in the
  world.
When the time came for him to be glorified by you, his
  heavenly Father,
he showed the depth of his love.

While they were at supper,
he took bread, said the blessing, broke the bread
and gave it to his disciples, saying:
Take this, all of you, and eat it:
this is my body which will be given up for you.
In the same way, he took the cup, filled with wine.
He gave you thanks, and giving the cup to his disciples,
  said:
Take this, all of you, and drink from it;
this is the cup of my blood,
the blood of the new and everlasting covenant.
It will be shed for you and for all men
so that sins may be forgiven.
Do this in memory of me.

Let us proclaim the mystery of faith:

ALL: Christ has died,
    Christ is risen,
    Christ will come again.

Alternatives

2. Dying you destroyed our death,
   rising you restored our life.
   Lord Jesus, come in glory.

3. When we eat this bread and drink this cup,
   we proclaim your death, Lord Jesus,
   until you come in glory.

4. Lord, by your cross and resurrection
   you have set us free.
   You are the Saviour of the world.

Father, we now celebrate this memorial of our
   redemption.
We recall Christ's death, his descent among the dead,
his resurrection, and his ascension to your right hand;
and, looking forward to his coming in glory, we offer
   you his body and blood,
the acceptable sacrifice which brings salvation to the
   whole world.

Lord, look upon this sacrifice which you have given to
   your Church;
and by your Holy Spirit, gather all who share this bread
   and wine
into the one body of Christ, a living sacrifice of praise.

Lord, remember those for whom we offer this sacrifice,
especially N. . . . our Pope,
N. . . . our bishop, and bishops and clergy everywhere.
   Remember those who take part in this offering,
those here present and all your people,
and all who seek you with a sincere heart.
Remember those who have died in the peace of Christ

and all the dead whose faith is known to you alone.
Father, in your mercy grant also to us, your children
to enter into our heavenly inheritance
in the company of the Virgin Mary, the Mother of God,
and your apostles and saints.
Then in your kingdom, freed from the corruption of
  sin and death,
we shall sing your glory with every creature through
  Christ our Lord,
through whom you give us everything that is good.

(*Now turn to page 102.*)

Mass in Latin

Only those parts of the Mass to which the congregation (C.) is invited to join the priest (P.) or respond are here given.

P. In nomine Patris, et Filii, et Spiritus Sancti.

C. Amen.

P. Gratia Domini nostri Jesu Christi, et caritas Dei, et communicatio Sancti Spiritus sit cum omnibus vobis.

or

P. Dominus vobiscum.

C. Et cum spiritu tuo.

P. Fratres, agnoscamus peccata nostra, ut apti simus ad sacra mysteria celebranda.

P. AND C. Confiteor Deo omnipotenti et vobis, fratres, quia peccavi nimis
cogitatione, verbo, opere et omissione:
mea culpa, mea culpa, mea maxima culpa.
Ideo precor beatam Mariam semper Virginem
omnes angelos et sanctos,
et vos, fratres, orare pro me
ad Dominum Deum nostrum.

P. Misereatur nostri omnipotens Deus
et, dimissis peccatis nostris,
perducat nos ad vitam aeternam.

c. Amen.

p. Kyrie, eleison.	c. Kyrie, eleison.
p. Christe, eleison.	c. Christe, eleison.
p. Kyrie, eleison.	c. Kyrie, eleison.

p. AND c. Gloria in excelsis Deo
et in terra pax hominibus bonae voluntatis.
Laudamus te,
benedicimus te,
adoramus te,
glorificamus te.
Gratias agimus tibi propter magnam gloriam tuam,
Domine Deus, Rex caelestis,
Deus Pater omnipotens.
Domine Fili unigenite, Jesus Christe,
Domine Deus, Agnus Dei, Filius Patris,
qui tollis peccata mundi, miserere nobis;
qui tollis peccata mundi, suscipe deprecationem
nostram.
Qui sedes ad dexteram Patris, miserere nobis.
Quoniam tu solus Sanctus, tu solus Dominus, tu
solus Altissimus,
Jesu Christe, cum Sancto Spiritu: in gloria
Dei Patris. Amen.

c. (*at the end of the prayer*) Amen.

*　　　*　　　*

p. (*at the end of the reading*) Verbum Domini.
c. Deo Gratias.
p. (*at the beginning of the Gospel*) Dominus vobiscum.
c. Et cum spiritu tuo.
p. Initium (*or*) Sequentia sancti Evangelii secundum N....
c. Gloria tibi Domine.
p. (*a the end of the Gospel*) Verbum Domini.

c. Laus tibi, Christe.

p. AND c. Credo in unum Deum,
Patrem omnipotentem, factorem caeli et terrae,
visibilium omnium et invisibilium.
Et in unum Dominum Jesum Christum,
Filium Dei unigenitum,
et ex Patre natum ante omnia saecula.
Deum de Deo, lumen de lumine, Deum verum de
Deo vero,
genitum, non factum, consubstantialem Patri:
per quem omnia facta sunt.
Qui propter nos homines et propter nostram salutem
descendit de caelis. (*All bow*)
Et incarnatus est de Spiritu Sancto
ex Maria Virgine, et homo factus est.
Crucifixus etiam pro nobis sub Pontio Pilato;
passus et sepultus est,
et resurrexit tertia die, secundum Scripturas,
et ascendit in caelum, sedet ad dexteram Patris.
Et iterum venturus est cum gloria, iudicare vivos
et mortuos,
cuius regni non erit finis.
Et in Spiritum Sanctum, Dominum et vivificantem:
qui ex Patre Filioque procedit.
Qui cum Patre et Filio simul adoratur et
conglorificatur:
qui locutus est per prophetas.
Et unam, sanctam, catholicam et apostolicam
Ecclesiam.
Confiteor unum baptisma in remissionem peccatorum.
Et expecto resurrectionem mortuorum,
et vitam venturi saeculi. Amen.

*   *   *

P. (*at the offering of the bread*) Benedictus es, Domine,
Deus universi, quia de tua largitate accepimus panem,
quem tibi offerimus,
fructum terrae et operis manuum hominum,
ex quo nobis fiet panis vitae.

C. Benedictus Deus in saecula.

P. (*at the offering of the chalice*) Benedictus es, Domine,
Deus universi, quia de tua largitate accepimus
vinum,
quod tibi offerimus,
fructum vitis et operis manuum hominum,
ex quo nobis fiet potus spiritualis.

C. Benedictus Deus in saecula.

P. Orate, fratres: ut meum ac vestrum sacrificium
acceptabile fiat apud Deum Patrem omnipotentem.

C. Suscipiat Dominus sacrificium de manibus tuis
ad laudem et gloriam nominis sui,
ad utilitatem quoque nostram
totiusque Ecclesiae suae sanctae.

C. (*At the conclusion of the prayer*) Amen.

*　　*　　*

P. Dominus vobiscum.

C. Et cum spiritu tuo.

P. Sursum corda.

C. Habemus ad Dominum.

P. Gratias agamus Domino Deo nostro.

C. Dignum et iustum est.

P. AND C. Sanctus, Sanctus, Sanctus Dominus Deus
Sabaoth.
Pleni sunt caeli et terra gloria tua.

Hosanna in excelsis.
Benedictus qui venit in nomine Domini.
Hosanna in excelsis.

P. (*after showing the chalice*) Mysterium fidei.

C. Mortem tuam annuntiamus, Domine,
et tuam resurrectionem confitemur, donec venias.
(*or*)
Quotiescumque manducamus panem hunc
et calicem bibimus,
mortem tuam annuntiamus, Domine, donec venias.
(*or*)
Salvator mundi, salva nos,
qui per crucem et resurrectionem tuam liberasti nos.

P. Per ipsum, et cum ipso, et in ipso,
est tibi Deo Patri omnipotenti,
in unitate Spiritus Sancti,
omnis honor et gloria
per omnia saecula saeculorum.

C. Amen.

*   *   *

P. Praeceptis salutaribus moniti,
et divina institutione formati,
audemus dicere:

P. AND C. Pater noster, qui es in caelis:
sanctificetur nomen tuum;
adveniat regnum tuum;
fiat voluntas tua, sicut in caelo, et in terra.
Panem nostrum quotidianum da nobis hodie;
et dimitte nobis debita nostra,
sicut et nos dimittimus debitoribus nostris;
et ne nos inducas in tentationem;
sed libera nos a malo.

P. . . . et adventum Salvatoris nostri Jesu Christi.

c. Quia tuum est regnum,
et potestas, et gloria
in saecula.

P. Domine Jesu Christe, qui dixisti. . . .
Qui vivis et regnas in saecula saeculorum.

c. Amen.

P. Pax Domini sit semper vobiscum.

c. Et cum spiritu tuo.

c. Agnus Dei, qui tollis peccata mundi: miserere nobis.
Agnus Dei, qui tollis peccata mundi: miserere nobis.
Agnus Dei, qui tollis peccata mundi: dona nobis
pacem.

P. (*holding the host towards the people*) Ecce Agnus
Dei, ecce qui tollit peccata mundi.
Beati qui ad cenam Agni vocati sunt.

P. AND c. Domine, non sum dignus, ut intres sub
tectum meum
sed tantum dic verbo
et sanabitur anima mea.

P. Corpus Christi.

c. Amen.

c. (*after the final prayer*) Amen.

P. Dominus vobiscum.

c. Et cum spiritu tuo.

P. Benedicat vos omnipotens Deus,
Pater, et Filius, et Spiritus Sanctus.

c. Amen.

P. Ite, missa est.

c. Deo gratias.

Praying after Communion

After Communion, priest and people sit in silence for a while. Just how one uses these moments is very much a matter for the individual to decide for himself. The questions given below are no more than suggestions which may be of help to those who are uncertain as to how they should pray at this time.

Who am I that the Lord has come to?
Who is he who is now united to me?
What should I say to the Father who has given me his Son?
What should I say to Jesus who lives in me?
What is his Spirit saying to me?
What return can I make to the Lord for all he has done for me?
Is there anyone for whom I have particularly promised to pray?
Are there any other requests I should make known to the Lord?

Psalm 148

Let heaven praise the Lord:
praise him, heavenly heights,
praise him, all his angels,
praise him, all his armies.

Praise him, sun and moon,
praise him, shining stars,
praise him, highest heavens,
and waters above the heavens!

Let them all praise the name of the Lord
at whose command they were created;
he has fixed them in their place for ever,
by an unalterable statute.

Let earth praise the Lord:
sea-monsters and all the deeps,
fire and hail, snow and mist,
gales that obey his decree,

mountains and hills,
orchards and forests,
wild animals and farm animals,
snakes and birds,

all kings on earth and nations,
princes, all rulers in the world,
young men and girls,
old people and children too.

Let them all praise the name of the Lord,
for his name and no other is sublime,
transcending earth and heaven in majesty,
raising the fortunes of his people,
to the praises of the devout,
of Israel, the people dear to him.

A Prayer (sometimes called *Prayer before a Crucifix*)

Behold, O kind and most sweet Jesus,
I cast myself on my knees in thy sight,
and with the most fervent desire of my soul, I pray and
    beseech thee,
that thou wouldst impress upon my heart lively senti-
    ments of faith, hope and charity, with a true repentance
    for my sins, and a firm desire of amendment,
while with deep affection and grief of soul I ponder
    within myself and mentally contemplate thy five most
    precious wounds,
having before my eyes that which spake in prophecy of
    thee,
O good Jesus, 'They pierced my hands and my feet;
    they have numbered all my bones.'

*Other prayers suitable for the time after Communion may
be found on pages 39 and 40.*

Benediction

Benediction is a devotional service in honour of Christ's sacramental presence in the Eucharist. The priest puts the Blessed Sacrament where it may be seen. After an opening hymn there may be a reading and a time of silence for reflection. Then the following hymn may be sung.

Therefore we before him bending
This great sacrament revere;
Types and shadows have their ending,
For the newer rite is here;
Faith, our outward sense befriending,
Makes the inward vision clear.

Glory let us give and blessing
To the Father and the Son;
Honour, might and praise addressing,
While eternal ages run;
Ever too his love confessing,
Who from both, with both is one.

PRIEST: You have given them bread from heaven

ALL: Containing in itself all sweetness.

PRIEST: Let us pray: O God, in this wonderful sacrament you have left us a memorial of your passion. Grant that we may so reverence the sacred mysteries of your body and blood, that we may always enjoy within ourselves the fruit of your redemption, you who live and reign for ever and ever.

ALL: Amen.

After the blessing priest and people together say the Divine Praises:

Blessed be God
Blessed be his holy name
Blessed be Jesus Christ, true God and true man
Blessed be the name of Jesus
Blessed be his most sacred heart
Blessed be his most precious blood
Blessed be Jesus in the most holy Sacrament of the altar
Blessed be the Holy Spirit, the Paraclete
Blessed be the great Mother of God, Mary most holy
Blessed be her holy and immaculate conception
Blessed be her glorious assumption
Blessed be the name of Mary, virgin and mother
Blessed be St Joseph, her spouse most chaste
Blessed be God in his angels and in his saints

Then a final hymn is sung.

The Sacrament of Matrimony

The Sacrament of Matrimony consecrates the unselfish love of a man for a woman, and a woman for a man. This love, given and received for each other's sake, not their own, and expressed in the day to day living with each other, reaches its climax when man and woman become 'one body' in the act of love. It is a holy act, a source of grace to themselves. Besides being an expression of their vowed love for each other, it may be that in this act they are cooperating with God's continuing creative activity, and that a child will be conceived.

The help that the sacrament gives to those who respond to the call (vocation) of marriage, is not limited to the day of the wedding. Its power is available to husband and wife throughout the whole of their married lives.

The family is the basic cell of human society. Unselfish love in the family will spread outwards and affect others in the community. Love in the community will spread outwards and affect the nation: the nation will affect the world.

Of ourselves we are incapable of maintaining this unselfish and world-transforming love. The atmosphere of selfishness inherited from the first human beings (increased by present sinfulness), stifles all love that depends for its endurance only on human

effort. The mighty power of God given in the Sacra-
ment of Matrimony alone makes husband and wife
able to persevere in this kind of loving.

This Sacrament is normally celebrated as part of
the Mass. After the Gospel the priest will give a talk
on the mystery of Christian marriage, the nobility
of married love and the responsibilities of marriage.

The Rite of Marriage

STAND

PRIEST: Dear Friends, you have come together in this
church so that the Lord may seal and strengthen your
love in the presence of the Church's minister and this
community. Christ abundantly blesses this love. He
has already consecrated you in baptism and now he
enriches and strengthens you by a special sacrament
so that you may assume the duties of marriage in
mutual and lasting fidelity. And so, in the presence of
the Church, I ask you to state your intentions.

N. . . . and N. . . . have you come here freely and
without reservation to give yourselves to each other in
marriage? Will you love and honour each other as man
and wife for the rest of your lives?

Will you accept children lovingly from God, and
bring them up according to the law of Christ and his
Church?

*(The last question may be omitted if the the couple are ad-
vanced in years.)*

Each answers the questions separately.

PRIEST: Since it is your intention to enter into marriage,
join your right hands, and declare your consent before
God and his Church.

BRIDEGROOM: I, *N.* . . . ., take you, *N.* . . . ., to be my wife. I promise to be true to you in good times and in bad, in sickness and in health. I will love and honour you all the days of my life.

BRIDE: I, *N.* . . . ., take you, *N.* . . . ., to be my husband. I promise to be true to you in good times and in bad, in sickness and in health. I will love and honour you all the days of my life.

Alternatively

PRIEST: *N.* . . . ., do you take *N.* . . . . to be your wife? Do you promise to be true to her in good times and in bad, in sickness and in health, and to love and honour her all the days of your life?

BRIDEGROOM: I do.

PRIEST: *N.* . . . ., do you take *N.* . . . ., to be your husband? Do you promise to be true to him in good times and bad, in sickness and health, and to love and honour him all the days of your life?

BRIDE: I do.

PRIEST: You have declared your consent before the Church. May the Lord in his goodness strengthen your consent and fill you both with his blessings.
What God has joined, men must not divide.

ALL: Amen.

PRIEST: May the Lord bless these rings
which you give to each other
as the sign of your love and fidelity.

ALL: Amen.

The bridegroom now takes the bride's ring and places it on her ring finger, and, if it is appropriate, says:

BRIDEGROOM: *N.* . . . ., take this ring as a sign of my love and fidelity. In the name of the Father and of the Son and of the Holy Spirit.

The Bride now takes the bridegroom's ring and places it on his ring finger.

BRIDE: *N.* . . . , take this ring as a sign of my love and fidelity. In the name of the Father and of the Son and of the Holy Spirit.

The Mass now continues in the usual form until the Lord's prayer. After the Our Father, the priest turns to the bridegroom and bride.

PRIEST: Dear friends, let us turn to the Lord and pray that he will bless with his grace this woman
now married in Christ to this man
and that (through the sacrament of the body and blood of Christ)
he will unite in love the couple he has joined in this holy bond. (*Pause.*)

Father, by your power you have made everything out of nothing.
In the beginning you created the universe
and made mankind in your own likeness.
You gave man the constant help of woman
so that man and woman should no longer be two but one flesh,
and you teach us that what you have united
may never be lawfully divided.

Father, you have made the union of man and wife a holy mystery
that it symbolises the marriage of Christ and his Church.

Father, by your plan, man and woman united
and married, life has been established
as the one blessing that was not forfeited by original sin
or washed away in the flood.

Look with love upon this woman, your daughter,
now joined to her husband in marriage.
She asks your blessing.
Give her the grace of love and peace.
May she always follow the example of the holy women
whose praises are sung in the scriptures.

May her husband put his trust in her
and recognise that she is his equal
and the heir with him to the life of grace.
May he always honour and love her
as Christ loves his bride, the Church.

Father, keep them always true to your commandments.
Keep them faithful in marriage
and let them be examples of Christian life.
Give them the strength which comes from the gospel
so that they may be witnesses of Christ to others.
(Bless them with children
and help them to be good parents.
May they live to see their children's children.)
And after a happy old age,
grant them fullness of life with the saints
in the kingdom of heaven
(We ask this) through Christ our Lord.

ALL: Amen.

Alternatives

2. Let us pray to the Lord for N... and N...
   who come to God's altar at the beginning of their
   married life
   so that they may always be united in love for each other
   (as now they share in the body and blood of Christ).

   (*Pause.*)

Holy Father, you created mankind in your own image
and made man and woman to be joined as husband and
   wife
in the union of body and heart
and so fulfil their mission in this world.
Father, to reveal the plan of your love,
you made the union of husband and wife
an image of the covenant between you and your people.
In the fulfilment of this sacrament,
the marriage of Christian man and woman
is a sign of the marriage between Christ and the Church
Father, stretch out your hand, and bless N. . . and N. . .

Lord, grant that as they begin to live this sacrament
they may share with each other the gifts of your love
and become one in heart and mind
as witnesses to your presence in their marriage.
Help them to create a home together,
(and give them children to be formed by the gospel,
and to have a place in your family.

Give your blessings to N. . . , your daughter,
so that she may be a good wife (and mother),
caring for the home,
faithful in love for her husband,
generous and kind.
Give your blessings to N. . . , your son,
so that he may be a faithful husband
(and a good father).

Father, grant that as they come together to your
table on earth, so they may one day have the joy of
sharing your feast in heaven. (We ask this) through
Christ our Lord.

ALL: Amen.

3. My dear friends, let us ask God

for his continued blessings upon this bridegroom and
his bride (or *N. . .* and *N. . .*).
(*Pause.*)

Holy Father, Creator of the universe,
maker of man and woman in your own likeness,
source of blessing for married life,
we humbly pray to you for this woman
who today is united with her husband in this sacrament of marriage.
May your fullest blessing come upon her and her
husband
so that they may together rejoice in your gift of married
love
(and enrich your Church with their children).
Lord, may they both praise you when they are happy
and turn to you in their sorrows.
May they be glad that you help them in their work
and know that you are with them in their need.
May they pray to you in the community of the Church
and be your witnesses in the world.
May they reach old age in the company of their friends
and come at last to the kingdom of heaven.
(We ask this) through Christ, our Lord.

ALL: Amen.

---

*At the end of Mass the couple receive the special marriage
blessing.*

PRIEST: God the eternal Father keep you in love with
each other
so that the peace of Christ may stay with you
and be always in your home.

ALL: Amen.

PRIEST: May you always bear witness to the love of God
in this world

so that the afflicted and the needy
will find in you generous friends.

ALL: Amen.

PRIEST: And may almighty God bless you all,
the Father and the Son and the Holy Spirit.

ALL: Amen.

Alternatives

2.

PRIEST: May God, the almighty Father,
give you his joy
and bless you
(in your children).

ALL: Amen.

PRIEST: May the only Son of God have mercy on you
and help you in good times and in bad.

ALL: Amen.

PRIEST: May the Holy Spirit of God
always fill your hearts with his love.

ALL: Amen.

PRIEST: And may almighty God bless you all,
the Father, and the Son and the Holy Spirit.

ALL: Amen.

3.

PRIEST: May the Lord Jesus who was a guest at the
wedding in Cana,
bless you and your families and friends.

ALL: Amen.

PRIEST: May Jesus, who loved his Church to the end, always fill your hearts with his love.

ALL: Amen.

PRIEST: May he grant that, as you believe in his resurrection
so you may wait for him in joy and love.

ALL: Amen.

PRIEST: And may almighty God bless you all,
the Father, and the Son, and the Holy Spirit.

ALL: Amen.

The Sacrament of Holy Order

The one mediator between God and man is Jesus Christ, our Lord. The ordained priest shares in a special way in the mediating work of Jesus, the great high priest.

The priest's main work is to preach the gospel, the good news of our salvation, and to lead men in the offering of the holy sacrifice of the Mass. The text of the ordination ceremony is usually provided for the congregation. The passage given below, part of the ordination ceremony, describes in some detail what the Church expects of her priests.

THE BISHOP: These men, our sons – who are your relatives or friends – are about to be raised to the order of priest. You should therefore consider carefully the position in the Church which they will have.

It is true that the entire people of God, as a holy people, constitutes a royal priesthood in Christ. Nevertheless, our high priest, Jesus Christ, chose certain disciples to undertake in his name the public ministry of priesthood in the church for the sake of others. As he was sent by the Father, he sent the apostles into the world so that through them and their successors, the bishops, he might continue for ever his work as teacher, priest and pastor. Priests are co-workers of the college of bishops since they are joined to the bishops in the priestly office and are called to serve the people of God.

Our brothers have seriously considered this step and are now to be ordained priests. They will serve Christ the teacher, priest and pastor whose ministry it is to make his own body, the church, grow into the people of God, a holy temple.

They are called to share in the priesthood of the bishops and to mould themselves in the likeness of Christ, the supreme and eternal priest. By consecration they will be made true priests of the New Testament who will preach the gospel, sustain the people of God, and celebrate sacred rites, especially the Lord's sacrifice.

My sons, you are about to be promoted to the order of priest. You must apply your energies to your sacred duty of instruction in the name of Christ who is the chief teacher. Share with all men that Word of God which you have received with joy. While you meditate on the law of the Lord, see that you believe what you read, that you teach what you believe, and that you translate your teaching into action.

Let your instruction serve as a nourishing diet for the people of God. Let the impact of your lives please the followers of Christ, so that by word and action you may strengthen the house which is the Church of God.

In the same way, you must carry out your mission of sanctifying the world in Christ. It is your ministry which will make the spiritual sacrifices of the faithful perfect by uniting them to the eucharistic sacrifice of Christ. That sacrifice of Christ will be offered sacramentally in an unbloody way through your hands. Understand the meaning of what you do; put into practice what you celebrate. When you recall the mystery of the death and resurrection of the Lord try to die to sin and to walk in the new life of Christ.

In baptising men, you will bring them into the people of God; in the sacrament of penance you will forgive sins in the name of Christ and the church; with holy oil you will relieve and console the sick. You will celebrate the liturgy, offer thanks and praise to God through every hour of the day, praying for the whole people of God and the whole world as well. As you do this, always keep in mind that you are a man chosen from among men and appointed to act for men in their relations with God. Do your part in the work of Christ the Priest with the unfailing gladness of genuine charity, and look after the concerns of Christ, not your own.

Finally, my dear sons, as far as in you lies, carry on the work of Christ, the head of the church and its pastor. Work in union and in harmony with your bishop, and try to bring the faithful together like a unified family so that you may lead them effectively through Christ and in the Holy Spirit to God the Father. Always remember the example of the good shepherd who came to serve rather than be served, to seek out and save what had gone astray.

Towards the end of the rite of ordination, the Bishop says this prayer of consecration:

We ask you, all-powerful Father, give these servants of yours, the dignity of the priesthood. Renew the spirit of holiness within them. By your divine gift may they attain the second order in the hierarchy and exemplify right conduct in their lives.

May they be our fellow-workers, so that the words of the gospel may reach the farthest parts of the earth, and all nations, gathered together in Christ, may become one holy people of God.

Through Jesus Christ, your Son, our Lord, who lives and reigns with you in the unity of the Holy Spirit, God for ever and ever. Amen.

Sacrament of the Sick

'If one of you is ill, he should send for the elders of the Church, and they must anoint him with oil in the name of the Lord and pray over him. The prayer of faith will save the sick man and the Lord will raise him up again; and if he has committed any sins, he will be forgiven.' (James 5, 14–15.)

The sacrament of the sick is for the very ill. The sacrament forgives the sins of those who are sorry, it removes fear and anxiety from those who have faith and trust, it may restore health if God so wills it.

Since this sacrament is usually preceded by confession and communion, this sequence is given below. The priest will quite often call on the house-bound who are not so seriously ill and celebrate the first two Sacraments only.

If it is possible, there should be by the bedside a crucifix, two blessed candles and a small glass of drinking water. The candles should be lit shortly before the priest is due; he should be met at the door and led to the sick room. Obviously the attendant should leave the sick room if the invalid should wish to confess and return only when the priest indicates.

PRIEST: Peace be upon this house.

RESPONSE: And upon all who dwell herein.

PRIEST (*sprinkling with holy water*): Sprinkle me with hyssop, O Lord, and I shall be cleansed. Wash me and I shall be made whiter than snow. Have mercy on me, O God, as thou art ever rich in mercy. Glory be to the Father, and to the Son and to the Holy Spirit.

RESPONSE: As it was in the beginning, is now and ever shall be, world without end. Amen.

PRIEST: Our help is in the name of the Lord.

RESPONSE: Who made heaven and earth.

PRIEST: Lord hear my prayer.

RESPONSE: And let my cry come to thee.

PRIEST: The Lord be with you.

RESPONSE: And also with you.

PRIEST: Let us pray: Graciously hear us, holy Lord and Father, almighty and eternal God, and in thy goodness send thy holy angel from heaven to watch over all who dwell in this house. May his coming put new heart in them; may he protect them and be with them to defend them from all harm. Through Christ our Lord. Amen.

The priest may now hear the sick person's confession. If the invalid is not sure how to make a confession, he need only say so to the priest who will help him. (See also pages 76 to 83.)

Then the sick person and the attendant may say: I confess to almighty God, and to you my brothers and sisters that I have sinned through my own fault, in my thoughts and in my words, in what I have done and in what I have failed to do; and I ask blessed Mary, ever Virgin, all the angels and saints, and you my brothers and sisters to pray for me to the Lord our God.

PRIEST: May Almighty God have mercy on you, forgive you your sins, and bring you to everlasting life.

RESPONSE: Amen.

PRIEST: May the almighty and merciful Lord grant you pardon, absolution and remission of your sins.

RESPONSE: Amen.

PRIEST (*holding the host to be seen by the sick person*): This is the Lamb of God who takes away the sins of the world. Happy are they who are called to his supper.

RESPONSE: Lord, I am not worthy to receive you; but only say the word and I shall be healed.

PRIEST (*as he gives Communion*): The Body of Christ.

RESPONSE: Amen.

PRIEST: Let us pray: Holy Lord, and Father, almighty and eternal God, we ask thee with full confidence that our brother (sister) may find an unfailing remedy for the ills of his (her) body and soul in receiving the sacred Body of our Lord, Jesus Christ, thy Son, who lives and reigns for ever.

RESPONSE: Amen.

The Anointing of the Sick Person

The priest stretches his hand over the head of the sick person and says: In the name of the Father and of the Son and of the Holy Spirit, may all the devil's power in you be extinguished as we lay our hands upon you, and call upon the glorious Mother of God, the blessed Virgin Mary, upon St Joseph, her glorious spouse, and upon the angels, archangels, patriarchs, prophets, apostles, martyrs, confessors, virgins, and all the saints together, to intercede for you. Amen.

The priest dips his thumb into holy oil and anoints the sick person in the form of a cross on eyelids, ears, nostrils, lips, hands, feet* saying: Through this holy anointing and his most tender mercy may the Lord forgive you whatever sins you have committed through your sense of sight (hearing, smell, taste, touch, walking). Amen.

Lord, have mercy. Christ, have mercy. Lord, have mercy.

Our Father . . .

PRIEST: Save thy servant.

RESPONSE: Who puts his (her) trust in thee, my God.

PRIEST: Send him (her) help from thy holy place, O Lord.

RESPONSE: And defend him (her) out of Sion.

(The word 'Sion' is symbolic of God's Church. So: 'Let help come to him from your Church.')

PRIEST: Be to him (her) a tower of strength.

RESPONSE: Against the face of the enemy.

PRIEST: May the enemy have no advantage over him (her).

RESPONSE: Nor the son of iniquity have power to hurt him (her).

PRIEST: Lord, hear my prayer.

RESPONSE: And let my cry come to thee.

PRIEST: The Lord be with you.

RESPONSE: And also with you.

PRIEST: Let us pray: Lord God, thou didst say through thy Apostle, James: Is any man sick among you? Let him call in the priests of the Church and let them pray

*the feet need not be anointed if it is inconvenient.

over him, anointing him with oil in the name of the Lord, and the prayer of faith shall save the sick man, and the Lord shall raise him up; and if he be in sins they shall be forgiven him. We earnestly ask therefore of thee, our Redeemer, to bring to this thy servant the grace of the Holy Spirit, as a healing remedy for all his ills. Bind up his wounds; forgive his sins; rid him of all anguish of mind and body. Restore in thy mercy full health to his body and soul, so that with thy help he may be well and able to take up his work again and his duties in life. Who lives and reigns for ever.

RESPONSE: Amen.

PRIEST: We beg of thee, O Lord, to turn thy eyes towards *N* . . . . thy servant, lying here weak and weary. Warm with new life the soul thou didst create in him (her); and if for his own good thou hast made him (her) suffer, let him now feel that thy healing hand has taken his suffering away.

RESPONSE: Amen.

PRIEST: Holy Lord and Father, almighty and eternal God, who dost pour into broken human bodies the healing grace of thy own blessing, and in a thousand ways dost show thy care for what thy hands have made, be good to us and draw near, as we call upon thy name. Deliver thy servant from his (her) sickness. Give him (her) health anew. Stretch out thy hand and set him (her) on his (her) feet again. Put strength into him (her) and keep him (her) safe under thy powerful protection. Give him (her) back again to thy holy Church; and may all henceforth be well with him (her). Through Christ our Lord.

RESPONSE: Amen.

Prayers for the Dying

The following prayers are taken from the Roman Ritual.

We commend to your keeping the soul of your servant, N...., O Lord, and we beg of you, Lord Jesus Christ, Saviour of the world, who came down to this earth in pity for him (her) to find a resting place for him (her) in the bosom of the patriarchs. Acknowledge him (her) as yours, dear Lord, for he (she) came from your hands, and was created by you alone, the living and true God, not by any false divinity. There is indeed no other God than you, nor anyone who can do the things that you can do.

Let his (her) soul be filled with joy, O Lord, as he (she) stands before you. Forget all his (her) past wrongdoing, and the excesses into which angry passions or evil desires have led him (her). For although he (she) sinned, he (she) did not deny you, but always believed firmly in the Father and the Son and the Holy Spirit. He (She) was zealous for God's honour and faithfully worshipped God who made all things.

Remember no more the sins of his (her) youth, O Lord, and the wrong he (she) did when he (she) knew no better, but be mindful of him (her) in the brightness of your glory, according to your great mercy.

May the heavens be opened to him (her). May the angels rejoice with him (her). Receive your servant, Lord, into your kingdom.

May Michael the holy archangel, worthy prince of the heavenly armies, receive him (her).

May the holy angels of God come to meet him (her) and lead him (her) into the heavenly Jerusalem.

May blessed Peter the apostle to whom the keys of the kingdom were given, open the gate to him (her).

May St Paul who was the chosen bearer of the Gospel be there to help him (her).

May St John, the chosen apostle of God, to whom were revealed the hidden things of heaven, intercede for him (her).

May all the apostles, to whom was granted authority to rule the church, pray for him (her). May all those saints of God intercede for him (her), those chosen souls who suffered torments in this world to defend the name of Christ. So may our Lord, Jesus Christ grant that when he (she) has cast off the shackles of the body, he (she) may come to the glory of the kingdom of heaven.

May Mary, the virgin mother of God, kind comforter of all in distress, commend to her Son the soul of this his servant, N.... May she be to him (her) at this moment a true mother; and thus may he (she) overcome the fear of death and go forward, happy and in her company, to the place he (she) has always longed for in his heavenly home.

Saint Joseph, patron of the dying, I come to you to ask your help. Earnestly I commend to you the soul of this servant, N...., now in his (her) agony. At your own happy passing Jesus and Mary stood near, a two-fold assurance of salvation. Through your intercession may he (she) be delivered from the snares of the devil and from everlasting death, and be found worthy of eternal happiness. Through Christ our Lord. Amen.

At the moment of death

If the sick person is able, he should say the holy name, Jesus.
An attendant may say the following prayers:

Into thy hands, O Lord, I commend my spirit. Lord Jesus, receive my soul. Holy Mary, pray for me.

Jesus, Mary and Joseph I give you my heart and my soul.

Jesus, Mary and Joseph assist me in my last agony.

Jesus, Mary and Joseph may I sleep and take my rest with you. Amen.

After death

Come to his (her) aid, every saint of God; go out to meet him (her) every angel of God. Take his (her) soul and offer it in the sight of God's majesty. May Christ who called you take you to himself, and may the angels lead you into Abraham's bosom. Take his (her) soul and offer it in the sight of God's majesty.

Eternal rest give to him (her), O Lord.
And let perpetual light shine upon him (her).
May he (she) rest in peace. Amen.

(*Other prayers are on page 26.*)

Part Three

THIRTY READINGS
FROM THE BIBLE

God speaks to us today in all sorts of ways: through the circumstances of our lives, the advice and example of friends, the things that happen to us.

However, his voice should be most audible when we read his book, the Bible. 'Why read the Bible? As well ask a child why he should listen to the words of his father when he tells him what he has planned for him, or a bride why she would want to listen to the words of her husband when he tells her how much he loves her.'*

Before you start to read, humbly tell God that you want to listen to him. 'Speak Lord, for your servant is listening.'

Read the text very slowly and thoughtfully, and ask yourself how it may apply to your life. It may be as well to read the text two or three times.

After reading, think over unhurriedly what it is you have read. Speak to God about it.

1. Kind and Compassionate

God is kind and compassionate; that is the lesson Jesus taught. He said that God is merciful and loving to all his children.

The word 'compassionate' describes the sympathy he has for all those in trouble. It is the word most often used to describe Jesus' character. St James begs his readers to wait patiently until his coming.

*From *God Speaks to Us* by Father Richards. This is an excellent and inexpensive introduction to understanding the Bible (Darton, Longman and Todd, London 1963).

We must try to be like Jesus and show sympathy for others.

Now be patient, brothers, until the Lord's coming. Think of a farmer: how patiently he waits for the precious fruit of the ground until it has had the autumn rains and the spring rains! You too have to be patient; do not lose heart, because the Lord's coming will be soon. Do not make complaints against one another, brothers, so as not to be brought to judgement yourselves; the Judge is already to be seen waiting at the gates. For your example, brothers, in submitting with patience, take the prophets who spoke in the name of the Lord; remember it is those who had endurance that we say are the blessed ones. You have heard of the patience of Job, and understood the Lord's purpose, realising that the Lord is kind and compassionate. (James 5, 7–11.)

2. Light of the Nations

The idea of light plays a big part in the plan of our salvation. From the beginning when God said 'Let there be light' this idea runs through the whole of scripture, particularly in the writings of Isaiah. The words of the first paragraph Jesus was later to use to describe himself.

I have appointed you as covenant of the people and light of the nations,
to open the eyes of the blind,
to free captives from prison,
and those who live in darkness from the dungeon.'

(Isaiah 42, 6-7.)

'The people that walked in darkness
has seen a great light;
on those who live in a land of deep shadow
a light has shone.'

(Isaiah 9, 10.)

'Arise, shine out, for your light has come,
the glory of the Lord is rising on you,
though night still covers the earth
and darkness the peoples.
Above you the Lord now rises
and above you his glory appears.
The nations come to your light
and kings to your dawning brightness.'

(Isaiah 60, 1-3.)

3. God is Close to Us

*God is very close to those who show their love for
others – so close that he lives in them. This 'God-in-
us-life' is called 'Grace'. This is how the Apostle
John wrote about it in one of his letters.*

My dear people,
since God has loved us so much,
we too should love one another.
No one has ever seen God;
but as long as we love one another
God will live in us.
We can know that we are living in him
and he is living in us
because he lets us share his Spirit.
We ourselves saw and we testify
that the Father sent his Son
as saviour of the world.
If anyone acknowledges that Jesus is the Son of God,

God lives in him, and he in God.
We ourselves have known and put our faith in
God's love towards ourselves.
God is love
and anyone who lives in love lives in God,
and God lives in him.   (1 John 4, 11–16.)

4. Mary Says Yes

*The familiar word 'Hail' has been more exactly
translated as 'Rejoice'. The news Mary is given is
the cause of her rejoicing as it is ours. God, in graciously loving her, enabled her to return that love so
that she is full of grace.*

*God freely calls Mary and she freely responds.
Her reply is a pattern for all Christians. She makes
a humble admission that she doesn't deserve to be the
object of God's favour and couples it with an attempt
to make sure she has understood.*

*Then she gives an unconditional reply, no quali-
fications, no reservations for herself. 'I want God's
will to be done.'*

In the sixth month the angel Gabriel was sent by God
to a town in Galilee called Nazareth, to a virgin be-
trothed to a man named Joseph, of the House of David;
and the virgin's name was Mary. He went in and said
to her, 'Rejoice, so highly favoured! The Lord is with
you.' She was deeply disturbed by these words and
asked herself what this greeting could mean, but the
angel said to her, 'Mary, do not be afraid; you have
won God's favour. Listen! You are to conceive and bear
a son, and you must name him Jesus. He will be great
and will be called Son of the Most High. The Lord
God will give him the throne of his ancestor David; he
will rule over the House of Jacob for ever and his reign

will have no end.' Mary said to the angel, 'But how can this come about, since I am a virgin?' 'The Holy Spirit will come upon you' the angel answered 'and the power of the Most High will cover you with its shadow. And so the child will be holy and will be called Son of God.' 'I am the handmaid of the Lord,' said Mary 'let what you have said be done to me.' And the angel left her. (Luke 1, 26–38.)

5. This is the Lamb of God

John the Baptist was second cousin to Jesus. John had his own disciples; when he saw Jesus coming towards him, he said to his disciples – 'Here's the Lamb of God. Here's the one who takes away the sins of the world.' Then he said these words:

He must grow greater,
I must grow smaller.
He who comes from above
is above all others;
he who is born of the earth
is earthly himself and speaks in an earthly way.
He who comes from heaven
bears witness to the things he has seen and heard,
even if his testimony is not accepted;
though all who do accept his testimony
are attesting the truthfulness of God,
since he whom God has sent
speaks God's own words. (John 3, 30–34.)

6. Cause of our Joy

If you have a chance to listen to the music from the 'Messiah' you will hear how Handel paints a musical picture of the announcement of the birth of Jesus to the shepherds.

They came to Bethlehem and related their vision
to the young mother. St Luke's words express how
she felt and how she thought about God's request
of her.

'Today in the town of David a saviour has been born to
you; he is Christ the Lord. And here is a sign for you:
you will find a baby wrapped in swaddling clothes and
lying in a manger.' And suddenly with the angel there
was a great throng of the heavenly host, praising God
and singing:

    'Glory to God in the highest heaven,
      and peace to men who enjoy his favour'.

Now when the angels had gone from them into heaven,
the shepherds said to one another, 'Let us go to Bethlehem and see this thing that has happened which the
Lord has made known to us'. So they hurried away and
found Mary and Joseph, and the baby lying in the
manger. When they saw the child they repeated what
they had been told about him, and everyone who heard
it was astonished at what the shepherds had to say. As
for Mary, she treasured all these things and pondered
them in her heart.   (Luke, 2 11-19.)

7. Have No Fear

How glad we feel when the sun breaks through the
clouds after a storm. We quickly find the light switch
when we enter a dark room. Light removes shadow
and doubt. We can see around us. We don't need to
be afraid. The writer of the Hymn of Tobit thought
about this. He wrote about the joy people feel,
especially when God sent his light, his Son, to the
world to remove shadows and fears about the future.
'Live as I do' Jesus said, 'love one another and love
God the Father and you need have no fear . . .'

'A bright light shall shine
over all the regions of the earth;
many nations shall come from far away,
from all the ends of the earth
to dwell close to the Holy name of the Lord God,
with gifts in their hands for the King of heaven.
Within you, generation after generation
shall proclaim their joy,
and the name of her who is Elect shall endure
through the generations to come.'   (Tobit 13, 12–17.)

When Jesus spoke to the people again, he said:
'I am the light of the world;
anyone who follows me will not be walking in the
dark; he will have the light of life'.   (John 8, 12.)

Truly Free

*Are you a slave? A slave to your habits? Every now
and again you need to check. Our Lord says he will
set us free. Free from being a slave to ourselves, our
passions, our own way. Free to be a true son. St Paul
made the same point in his letter to the Christians in
Rome, many of whom were slaves.*

To the Jews who believed in him Jesus said:
'If you make my word your home
you will indeed be my disciples,
you will learn the truth
and the truth will make you free'.   (John 8, 31–32.)

Now, [however, you have been set free from sin, you
have been made slaves of God, and you get a reward
leading to your sanctification and ending in eternal life.
For the wage paid by sin is death; the present given by
God is eternal life in Christ Jesus our Lord.

(Romans 6, 22–23.)

9. Not a Soft Option

Being a christian isn't easy. It isn't meant to be. If you find no difficulty in being a christian, then it may mean that you are not following too closely in Christ's footsteps.

Then Jesus said to his disciples, 'If anyone wants to be a follower of mine, let him renounce himself and take up his cross and follow me. For anyone who wants to save his life will lose it; but anyone who loses his life for my sake will find it. What, then, will a man gain if he wins the whole world and ruins his life? Or what has a man to offer in exchange for his life?

(Matthew 16, 24–26.)

Anyone who loves his life loses it;
anyone who hates his life in this world
will keep it for the eternal life.
If a man serves me, he must follow me,
wherever I am, my servant will be there too.
If anyone serves me, my Father will honour him.

(John 12, 25–27.)

10. Unload All Your Worries

When we think of Christ carrying his cross, we remember how lovingly he spoke to those who were over burdened with cares and worries. 'Come unto me all you who are heavy laden.'

I really matter to God. He knows me by my name, and He will make the load lighter. St Peter echoes this idea in one of his short letters.

Wrap yourselves in humility to be servants of each other, because God refuses the proud and will always favour the humble. Bow down, then, before the power of God now, and he will raise you up on the appointed day; unload all your worries on to him, since he is looking after you. Be calm but vigilant, because your enemy the devil is prowling round like a roaring lion, looking for someone to eat. Stand up to him, strong in faith and in the knowledge that your brothers all over the world are suffering the same things. You will have to suffer only for a little while: the God of all grace who called you to eternal glory in Christ will see that all is well again: he will confirm, strengthen and support you. His power lasts for ever and ever. Amen.   (1 Peter 5, 5–11.)

11. A Call for Help

A person who is dying often recalls memories of his childhood. Possibly Jesus in his last agony remembered one of the Psalms learnt at his mother's side – Psalm 22 was quoted by him during the passion. It starts in despair, but the ending is triumphant.

'My God, my God, why have you deserted me?
How far from saving me, the words I groan!
I call all day, my God, but you never answer,
all night long I call and cannot rest.
Yet, Holy one, you
who make your home in the praises of Israel,
in you our fathers put their trust,
they trusted and you rescued them;
they called to you for help and they were saved;
they never trusted you in vain.
Yet here am I, now more worm than man.
scorn of mankind, jest of the people,
all who see me jeer at me,
they toss their heads and sneer,
"He relied on the Lord, let the Lord save him!
If God is his friend, let him rescue him".

*   *   *

I am like water draining away,
my bones are all disjointed,
my heart is like wax,
melting inside me;
my palate is drier than a potsherd
and my tongue is stuck to my jaw.

* * *

I can count every one of my bones,
and there they glare at me, gloating;
they divide my garments among them
and cast lots for my clothes.

Do not stand aside, Lord.
O my strength, come quickly to my help;
rescue my soul from the sword,
my dear life from the paw of the dog,
save me from the lion's mouth,
my poor soul from the wild bulls' horns!

Then I shall proclaim your name to my brothers,
praise you in full assembly:
you who fear the Lord, praise him!
Entire race of Jacob, glorify him!
Entire race of Israel, revere him!

For he has not despised
or disdained the poor man in his poverty,
has not hidden his face from him,
but has answered him when he called.

* * *

The whole earth, from end to end, will remember and
come back to the Lord;
all the families of the nations will bow down before him.
For the Lord reigns, the ruler of nations!

Before him all the prosperous of the earth will bow down,
before him will bow all who go down to the dust.
And my soul will live for him, my children will serve
    him;
men will proclaim the Lord to generations still to come,
his righteousness to a people yet unborn. All this he has
    done.'   (From Ps. 22.)

12. Jesus is Our Lord

*Jesus was sent by the Father to save us. He became a
man like ourselves in every way, except sin. He knew
that the longer he carried on trying to bring people
to know and love his Father, the more men would
turn against him. Eventually they would put him to
death. Even so he didn't give up. He stayed obedient,
and so God his Father raised him up and made him
glorious.*

His state was divine,
yet he did not cling
to his equality with God
but emptied himself
to assume the condition of a slave,
and became as men are;
and being as all men are,
he was humbler yet,
even to accepting death,
death on a cross.
But God raised him high
and gave him the name
which is above all other names
so that all beings
in the heavens, on earth and in the underworld,
should bend the knee at the name of Jesus

and that every tongue should acclaim
Jesus Christ as Lord,
to the glory of God the Father.   (Philippians 2, 6–11.)

13. This is Your Mother

Those who stood by the Cross included:

Clopas – he may have been St Joseph's brother.

Mary – the wife of Clopas, and so could have been our Lady's sister-in-law.

John – the author of this passage and the one referred to here as 'the disciple Jesus loved'.

Salome – (mentioned not in this Gospel but in Mark's) – John's mother.

If Jesus, in saying, 'Woman, this is your son', had simply been asking Mary, his mother, to be a mother also to John, he would have undoubtedly hurt the feelings of John's physical mother, Salome, standing close by. Jesus is therefore meaning something much deeper than that. Many Christians have believed that in the person of John, Jesus was presenting all his friends to his own mother Mary and asking her at this supreme moment to be a mother to them all.

Near the cross of Jesus stood his mother and his mother's sister, Mary the wife of Clopas, and Mary of Magdala. Seeing his mother and the disciple he loved standing near her, Jesus said to his mother, 'Woman, this is your son'. Then to the disciple he said, 'This is your mother'. And from that moment the disciple made a place for her in his home.   (John 19, 25–27.)

14. Jesus is Alive Today

In this letter to the Christians at Corinth, Paul sums up the heart of Christian faith and hope. After a quiet recording of the resurrection facts, he declares 'if Christ has not been raised up, our preaching is useless, and your believing it is useless'. If Jesus Christ hadn't come to life again, we are without faith and hope. The main challenge of our Faith is that Jesus is alive and close to us today.

Well then, in the first place, I taught you what I had been taught myself, namely that Christ died for our sins, in accordance with the scriptures; that he was buried; and that he was raised to life on the third day, in accordance with the scriptures; that he appeared first to Cephas and secondly to the Twelve. Next he appeared to more than five hundred of the brothers at the same time, most of whom are still alive, though some have died; then he appeared to James, and then to all the apostles; and last of all he appeared to me too; it was as though I was born when no one expected it . . .

Now if Christ raised from the dead is what has been preached, how can some of you be saying that there is no resurrection of the dead? If there is no resurrection of the dead, Christ himself cannot have been raised, and if Christ has not been raised then our preaching is useless and your believing it is useless . . .

If our hope in Christ has been for this life only, we are the most unfortunate of all people.

But Christ has in fact been raised from the dead, the first-fruits of all who have fallen asleep.

(Extracts from 1 Corinthians 15.)

15. Lord of All

Here is a lesser known summary of Christ's life, passion and death, and resurrection. It comes in the Acts of the Apostles. St Peter recounts the life of Jesus to a Roman centurion and his family, who had asked for the good news. The good news is that Jesus is alive today and is working through his church.

'It is true, God sent his word to the people of Israel, and it was to them that the good news of peace was brought by Jesus Christ – but Jesus Christ is Lord of all men. You must have heard about the recent happenings in Judaea; about Jesus of Nazareth and how he began in Galilee, after John had been preaching baptism. God had anointed him with the Holy Spirit and with power, and because God was with him, Jesus went about doing good and curing all who had fallen into the power of the devil. Now I, and those with me, can witness to everything he did throughout the countryside of Judaea and in Jerusalem itself: and also to the fact that they killed him by hanging him on a tree, yet three days afterwards God raised him to life and allowed him to be seen, not by the whole people but only by certain witnesses God had chosen beforehand. Now we are those witnesses – we have eaten and drunk with him after his resurrection from the dead.   (Acts 10, 36–42.)

16. Stay With Us Lord

St Luke tells of a meal Jesus had with two of his disciples on the day of his resurrection.

That very same day, two of them were on their way to a village called Emmaus, seven miles from Jerusalem, and they were talking together about all that had happened. Now as they talked this over, Jesus himself came up and walked by their side; but something prevented them from recognising him. He said to them, 'What matters are you discussing as you walk along?' They stopped short, their faces downcast.

Then one of them, called Cleopas, answered him. 'You must be the only person staying in Jerusalem who does not know the things that have been happening there these last few days'. 'What things?' he asked. 'All about Jesus of Nazareth' they answered 'who proved he was a great prophet by the things he said and did in the sight of God and of the whole people; and how our chief priests and our leaders handed him over to be sentenced to death, and had him crucified. Our own hope had been that he would be the one to set Israel free. And this is not all: two whole days have gone by since it all happened; and some women from our group have astounded us: they went to the tomb in the early morning, and when they did not find the body, they came back to tell us they had seen a vision of angels who declared he was alive. Some of our friends went to the tomb and found everything exactly as the women had reported, but of him they saw nothing.'

Then he said to them. 'You foolish men! So slow to believe the full message of the prophets! Was it not ordained that the Christ should suffer and so enter into his glory?' Then, starting with Moses and going through all the prophets, he explained to them the passages throughout the scriptures that were about himself.

When they drew near to the village to which they were going, he made as if to go on; but they pressed him to stay with them. 'It is nearly evening' they said 'and the day is almost over.' So he went in to stay with them. Now while he was with them at table, he took the bread and said the blessing; then he broke it and handed it to them. And their eyes were opened and they recognised him; but he had vanished from their sight. Then they said to each other, 'Did not our hearts burn within us as he talked to us on the road and explained the scriptures to us?'

(Luke 24, 13–32.)

17. The Spirit Who Unites

After the Resurrection Jesus sent his Spirit to men.

It is this spirit that keeps us united closely to Jesus
and closely to each other. Because of the Spirit we
are as close to Jesus today as the apostles were in
Palestine.

If you love me you will keep my commandments.
I shall ask the Father,
and he will give you another Advocate
to be with you for ever,
that Spirit of truth
whom the world can never receive
since it neither sees nor knows him;
but you know him,
because he is with you, he is in you.
I will not leave you orphans;
I will come back to you.   (John 14, 15–18.)

Yet you are sad at heart because I have told you this.
Still, I must tell you the truth:
it is for your own good that I am going
because unless I go,
the Advocate will not come to you;
but if I do go,
I will send him to you.   (John 16, 6–7.)

While Peter was still speaking the Holy Spirit came
down on all the listeners. Jewish believers who had
accompanied Peter were all astonished that the gift of
the Holy Spirit should be poured out on the pagans too,
since they could hear them speaking strange languages
and proclaiming the greatness of God. Peter himself
then said, 'Could anyone refuse the water of baptism to
these people, now they have received the Holy Spirit
just as much as we have?' He then gave orders for them
to be baptised in the name of Jesus Christ. Afterwards they
begged him to stay on for some days.   (Acts 10, 44–48.)

18. The Power of God

The enormous power of God in raising Jesus from the dead is beyond human comprehension, yet St Paul prays here that the people of Ephesus will have the Holy Spirit to help them to appreciate and share in this same power. Paul promises hope for those who believe in God's strength.

Mankind needs this hope today, as he sees his fellow men reaching out for power, harnessing nuclear energy, for evil as well as good.

May the God of our Lord Jesus Christ, the Father of glory, give you a spirit of wisdom and perception of what is revealed, to bring you to full knowledge of him. May he enlighten the eyes of your mind so that you can see what hope his call holds for you, what rich glories he has promised the saints will inherit and how infinitely great is the power that he has exercised for us believers. This you can tell from the strength of his power at work in Christ, when he used it to raise him from the dead and to make him sit at his right hand, in heaven, far above every Sovereignty, Authority, Power, or Domination, or any other name that can be named, not only in this age but also in the age to come.

(Ephesians 1, 17–22.)

19. The Bread of Life

The reading is taken from Jesus' Sermon on the bread of life, given at about the time of the Passover, a year before he died. He tells us how he can completely satisfy all our desires.

I am the bread of life.
He who comes to me will never be hungry;
he who believes in me will never thirst.

But, as I have told you,
you can see me and still you do not believe.
All that the Father gives me will come to me,
and whoever comes to me
I shall not turn him away;
because I have come from heaven,
not to do my own will,
but to do the will of the one who sent me.

(John 6, 35–38.)

20. Love Is ...

St Paul wrote these words to christians living in the port of Corinth. Corinth was one of the most vice-ridden cities in the world, and the Christians there were all recent converts. Given such circumstances to live a truly christian life would be most difficult. Some have said that in place of the word 'Love' in the following passage, one can insert the name 'Jesus'. One should be able to insert 'the follower of Jesus'.

Love is always patient and kind; it is never jealous; love is never boastful or conceited; it is never rude or selfish; it does not take offence, and is not resentful. Love takes no pleasure in other people's sins but delights in the truth; it is always ready to excuse, to trust, to hope, and to endure whatever comes.

Love does not come to an end. But if there are gifts of prophecy, the time will come when they must fail; or the gift of languages, it will not continue for ever; and knowledge – for this, too, the time will come when it must fail. For our knowledge is imperfect and our prophesying is imperfect; but once perfection comes, all imperfect things will disappear. When I was a child, I used to talk like a child, and think like a child, and argue like a child, but now I am a man, all childish ways are put behind me. Now we are seeing a dim reflection in a mirror; but then we shall be seeing face to face. The knowledge that I have now is imperfect; but then I shall know as fully as I am known.

In short, there are three things that last; faith, hope and love; and the greatest of these is love.

(1 Corinthians 13, 4–13.)

21. Watch Yourselves!

Jesus lived at a time when suffering, in the forms of sickness and physical handicap, was almost incurable. He took pity on those who suffered in this way. But he also showed pity to the sinners and he gave them a new start in life by forgiving them their sins.

In this passage he tells his followers to do the same. Keep giving people the chance to try by forgiving them continually. Seven times a day is the way St Luke puts it, he means time and time again, not only seven occasions. 'Forgive us our trespasses as we forgive those who trespass against us.'

The warning 'watch yourselves' needs to be heeded. What obstacles lead little ones astray today?

He said to his disciples, 'Obstacles are sure to come, but alas for the one who provides them! It would be better for him to be thrown into the sea with a millstone put around his neck than that he should lead astray a single one of these little ones. Watch yourselves!

'If your brother does something wrong, reprove him and, if he is sorry, forgive him. And if he wrongs you seven times a day and seven times comes back to you and says, "I am sorry", you must forgive him.'

(Luke 17, 1–4.)

22. Your Faith Has Saved You

Authority is the keynote of Jesus' healing words in this passage, yet behind that authority is Love. To him all men were equal if they were suffering. Christ cured only those who already had faith. If people did not have faith in him he could not help them.

It is the same today when we meet him in the sacraments. He helps us according to our faith in Him and our trust that he will help us. It is our faith/trust that saves us.

Jesus left Jericho with his disciples and a large crowd. Bartimaeus (that is, the son of Timaeus), a blind beggar, was sitting at the side of the road. When he heard that it was Jesus of Nazareth, he began to shout and to say, 'Son of David, Jesus, have pity on me'. And many of them scolded him and told him to keep quiet, but he only shouted all the louder, 'Son of David, have pity on me'. Jesus stopped and said, 'Call him here'. So they called the blind man. 'Courage,' they said 'get up; he is calling you.' So throwing off his cloak, he jumped up and went to Jesus. Then Jesus spoke, 'What do you want me to do for you?' 'Rabboni,' the blind man said to him 'Master, let me see again.' Jesus said to him, 'Go; your faith has saved you'. And immediately his sight returned and he followed him along the road.

(Mark 10, 46–52.)

23. When Did We See You?

Nothing has changed since Jesus first said these words. Read them again and ask yourself the questions asked here.

'When the Son of Man comes in his glory, escorted by all the angels, then he will take his seat on his throne of glory. All the nations will be assembled before him and he will separate men one from another as the shepherd separates sheep from goats. He will place the sheep on his right hand and the goats on his left. Then the King will say to those on his right hand, "Come, you whom my Father has blessed, take for your heritage the kingdom prepared for you since the foundation of the world. For I was hungry and you gave me food; I was thirsty and you gave me drink; I was a stranger and you made me welcome; naked and you clothed me, sick and you visited me, in prison and you came to see me." Then the virtuous will say to him in reply, "Lord, when did we see you hungry and feed you; or thirsty and give you drink? When did we see you a stranger and make you welcome; naked and clothe you; sick or in prison and go to see you?" And the King will answer, "I tell you solemnly, in so far as you did this to one of the least of these brothers of mine, you did it to me". Next he will say to those on his left hand, "Go away from me, with your curse upon you, to the eternal fire prepared for the devil and his angels. For I was hungry and you never gave me food; I was thirsty and you never gave me anything to drink; I was a stranger and you never made me welcome, naked and you never clothed me, sick and in prison and you never visited me." Then it will be their turn to ask, "Lord, when did we see you hungry or thirsty, a stranger or naked, sick or in prison, and did not come to your help?" Then he will answer, "I tell you solemnly, in so far as you neglected to do this to one of the least of these, you neglected to do it to me". And they will go away to eternal punishment, and the virtuous to eternal life.'

(Matthew 25, 31–46.)

24. 'I Am the Resurrection and the Life'

*This story reveals so much of the character of Jesus.
The tears he wept because his friend had died show
how human he was. His divinity can be seen in the
power he used to raise Lazarus to life. His sympathy
for people is also in evidence. Notice how Martha
and Mary say the same thing to him. But he uses
a different approach with each of them because of
their different characters. With Martha he reasons;
with Mary he weeps.*

On arriving, Jesus found that Lazarus had been in the
tomb for four days already. Bethany is only about two
miles from Jerusalem, and many Jews had come to
Martha and Mary to sympathise with them over their
brother. When Martha heard that Jesus had come she
went to meet him. Mary remained sitting in the house.
Martha said to Jesus, 'If you had been here, my brother
would not have died, but I know that, even now, whatever you ask of God, he will grant you.' 'Your brother'
said Jesus to her 'will rise again.' Martha said, 'I know
he will rise again at the resurrection on the last day'.
Jesus said:

> 'I am the resurrection.
> If anyone believes in me, even though he dies he
>   will live
> and whoever lives and believes in me
> will never die.
> Do you believe this?'

'Yes, Lord,' she said 'I believe that you are the Christ,
the Son of God, the one who was to come into this
world.'

When she had said this, she went and called her sister
Mary, saying in a low voice, 'The Master is here and

wants to see you'. Hearing this, Mary got up quickly and went to him. Jesus had not yet come into the village; he was still at the place where Martha had met him. When the Jews who were in the house sympathising with Mary saw her get up so quickly and go out, they followed her, thinking that she was going to the tomb to weep there.

Mary went to Jesus, and as soon as she saw him she threw herself at his feet, saying, 'Lord, if you had been here, my brother would not have died'. At the sight of her tears, and those of the Jews who followed her, Jesus said in great distress, with a sigh that came straight from the heart, 'Where have you put him?' They said, 'Lord, come and see'. Jesus wept; and the Jews said, 'See how much he loved him!' But there were some who remarked, 'He opened the eyes of the blind man, could he not have prevented this man's death?' Still sighing, Jesus reached the tomb: it was a cave with a stone to close the opening. Jesus said, 'Take the stone away'. Martha said to him, 'Lord, by now he will smell; this is the fourth day'. Jesus replied, 'Have I not told you that if you believe you will see the glory of God?' So they took away the stone. Then Jesus lifted up his eyes and said:

'Father, I thank you for hearing my prayer.
I knew indeed that you always hear me,
but I speak
for the sake of all these who stand round me,
so that they may believe it was you who sent me.'

When he had said this, he cried in a loud voice, 'Lazarus, here! Come out!' The dead man came out, his feet and hands bound with bands of stuff and a cloth round his face. Jesus said to them, 'Unbind him, let him go free'. (John 11, 17–44.)

25. Who is my Neighbour?

Can we be bothered to put ourselves out for others?
People can't always avoid falling on bad times.
When they do, the 'Samaritan' is ready to listen to
their problem, give a helping hand, find ways of taking
care of them if necessary.

Who is my neighbour? The refugee, the prisoner,
the homeless, the mentally sick, the aged, the alco-
holic, the widow, the hungry, the physically handi-
capped, those whose marriages have failed – the list
is limitless.

Jesus carefully chose the individual he wanted to
portray as a true neighbour. He picked a Samaritan,
someone who belonged to a race his listeners hated
and despised!

A lawyer anxious to justify himself said to Jesus, 'And
who is my neighbour?' Jesus replied, 'A man was once
on his way down from Jerusalem to Jericho and fell into
the hands of brigands; they took all he had, beat him
and then made off, leaving him half dead. Now a priest
happened to be travelling down the same road, but when
he saw the man, he passed by on the other side. In the
same way a Levite who came to the place saw him, and
passed by on the other side. But a Samaritan traveller
who came upon him was moved with compassion when
he saw him. He went up and bandaged his wounds,
pouring oil and wine on them. He then lifted him on
to his own mount, carried him to the inn and looked
after him. Next day, he took out two denarii and handed
them to the innkeeper. "Look after him," he said "and
on my way back I will make good any extra expense
you have." Which of these three, do you think, proved
himself a neighbour to the man who fell into the brigands'

hands?' 'The one who took pity on him' he replied.
Jesus said to him, 'Go, and do the same yourself'.

(Luke 10, 29–37.)

26. We Shall Be One

Jesus said these words after his last supper with his
friends. Possibly as they walked away from the
supper-room towards the garden of Gethsemane,
Jesus pointed to a vine growing by the side of the path.
His friends were confused: they did not know what
he meant when he said he was going away, and yet
would still be united to them. Jesus pointed to the
vine, and said – 'This is how we will always be close
together.'

'I am the true vine,
and my Father is the vinedresser.
Every branch in me that bears no fruit
he cuts away,
and every branch that does bear fruit he prunes
to make it bear even more.
You are pruned already,
by means of the word that I have spoken to you.
Make your home in me, as I make mine in you.
As a branch cannot bear fruit all by itself,
but must remain part of the vine,
neither can you unless you remain in me.
I am the vine,
you are the branches.
Whoever remains in me, with me in him,
bears fruit in plenty;
for cut off from me you can do nothing.
Anyone who does not remain in me
is like a branch that has been thrown away
– he withers;

these branches are collected and thrown on the fire,
and they are burnt.
If you remain in me
and my words remain in you,
you may ask what you will
and you shall get it.'　　　　　　　　　　(John 15, 1–7.)

27. The Good News of Jesus

*The word 'Gospel' means 'Good News'. The greatest
news we ever had was that God sent his Son Jesus
to save us.*

*I am linked to Jesus by the fact that I am
baptised. This should make me happy. It had that
effect on the Ethiopian who 'went on his way
rejoicing'.*

*A Missionary said that Africans love this story
for it tells how one of their own people became one of
the first Christians.*

Philip set off on his journey. Now it happened that
an Ethiopian had been on pilgrimage to Jerusalem; he
was a eunuch and an officer at the court of the kandake, or
queen, of Ethiopia, and was in fact her chief treasurer.
He was now on his way home; and as he sat in his chariot
he was reading the prophet Isaiah. The Spirit said to
Philip, 'Go up and meet that chariot'. When Philip ran
up, he heard him reading Isaiah the prophet and asked,
'Do you understand what you are reading?' 'How can
I' he replied 'unless I have someone to guide me?' So
he invited Philip to get in and sit by his side. Now the
passage of scripture he was reading was this:

Like a sheep that is led to the slaughter-house,
like a lamb that is dumb in front of its shearers,
like these he never opens his mouth.
He has been humiliated and has no one to defend him.

Who will ever talk about his descendants,
since his life on earth has been cut short!

The eunuch turned to Philip and said, 'Tell me, is the prophet referring to himself or someone else?' Starting, therefore, with this text of scripture Philip proceeded to explain the Good News of Jesus to him.

Further along the road they came to some water, and the eunuch said, 'Look, there is some water here; is there anything to stop me being baptised?' He ordered the chariot to stop, then Philip and the eunuch both went down into the water and Philip baptised him. But after they had come up out of the water again Philip was taken away by the Spirit of the Lord, and the eunuch never saw him again but went on his way rejoicing. Philip found that he had reached Azotus and continued his journey proclaiming the Good News in every town as far as Caesarea.   (Acts 8, 27–40.)

28. Alive for God

There is a new life surging in us because we are baptised; the life of God himself. The converts Paul was writing to in Rome could well remember the kind of people they were before Baptism. Paul asked his readers to 'be alive for God'.

A Christian realises that he can live out his Baptism every day by finishing with sin and living for God.

You have been taught that when we were baptised in Christ Jesus we were baptised in his death; in other words, when we were baptised we went into the tomb with him and joined him in death, so that as Christ was raised from the dead by the Father's glory, we too might live a new life.

If in union with Christ we have imitated his death, we shall also imitate him in his resurrection. We must realise that our former selves have been crucified with him to destroy this sinful body and to free us from the slavery of sin. When a man dies, of course, he has finished with sin.

But we believe that having died with Christ we shall return to life with him: Christ, as we know, having been raised from the dead will never die again. Death has no power over him any more. When he died, he died, once for all, to sin, so his life now is life with God; and in that way, you too must consider yourselves to be dead to sin but alive for God in Christ Jesus.

(Romans 6, 3–11.)

29. We Are Not Alone

This passage is a consolation to anyone who is going through a period of distress or trouble. It is a consequence of life, part of being a human being. But we have a great power behind us – so that even though the world seems to be falling apart, we can triumph. We are more than conquerors because of the power of God.

With God on our side who can be against us? Since God did not spare his own Son, but gave him up to benefit us all, we may be certain, after such a gift, that he will not refuse anything he can give. Could anyone accuse those that God has chosen? When God acquits, could anyone condemn? Could Christ Jesus? No! He not only died for us – he rose from the dead, and there at God's right hand he stands and pleads for us.

Nothing therefore can come between us and the love of Christ, even if we are troubled or worried, or being persecuted, or lacking food or clothes, or being threatened or even attacked. As scripture promised: For your sake we are being massacred daily, and reckoned as sheep for the slaughter. These are the trials through which we triumph, by the power of him who loved us.

For I am certain of this: neither death nor life, no angel, no prince, nothing that exists, nothing still to come, not any power, or height or depth, nor any created thing, can ever come between us and the love of God made visible in Christ Jesus our Lord.

(Romans 8, 31–39.)

30. Glory to Him

To affirm that God's power can do more for us than we would dream of asking is the reason for Paul's prayer in this letter to the Christians at Ephesus. But it depends on our growth in love. That is the answer to our continual search for happiness and security.

This, then, is what I pray, kneeling before the Father, from whom every family, whether spiritual or natural, takes its name:

Out of his infinite glory, may he give you the power through his Spirit for your hidden self to grow strong, so that Christ may live in your hearts through faith, and then, planted in love and built on love, you will with all the saints have strength to grasp the breadth and the length, the height and the depth; until, knowing the love of Christ, which is beyond all knowledge, you are filled with the utter fullness of God.

Glory be to him whose power, working in us, can do infinitely more than we can ask or imagine; glory be to him from generation to generation in the Church and in Christ Jesus for ever and ever. Amen.

(Ephesians 3, 14–21.)

Part Four

THE LITURGICAL SEASONS

The Christmas Season

Preparation

In the northern hemisphere the feast of Christmas occurs just after the shortest day in the year. December 25th promises a return to lighter days. So it is appropriate that at this time we should honour the birthday of the light of the world. In the four weeks of advent we make ourselves ready for Christmas. By recalling the first coming of Christ in weakness and humility, we prepare for his second coming in power and glory – the parousia.

A PRAYER FOR ADVENT

Father, all-powerful and ever-living God,
we do well always and everywhere to give you thanks
through Jesus Christ our Lord.

His future coming was proclaimed by all the prophets.
The virgin mother bore him in her womb with love
    beyond all telling.
John the Baptist was his herald
and made him known when at last he came.

In his love he has filled us with joy
as we prepare to celebrate his birth,
so that when he comes he may find us watching in prayer,
our hearts filled with wonder and praise.

Preface for Advent II.

Let us pray: Lord Jesus, stir up your power and come. Deliver us from all the dangers of our sinfulness.

O God, our Father, we are preparing to celebrate the birthday of your Son, Jesus Christ. While we recall his coming as a tiny baby in weakness and humility, may we be reminded that one day he will come in power and glory. We make this prayer to you through the same Jesus Christ, your Son, who lives and reigns with you in the unity of the Holy Spirit, for ever and ever. Amen.

Readings for Advent will be found on pp. 159–163.

The Celebration

The Celebration of Christmas begins with midnight Mass and ends on January 6th, the Epiphany.

Christmas is traditionally the time of gift-giving because Jesus is the supreme gift from the Father to mankind. 'Yes, God loved the world so much that he gave his only Son, so that everyone who believes in him may have eternal life.' (John 3, 16.)

Jesus' parents were temporarily homeless when he was born. At Christmas time our thoughts should turn to the unfortunate: the homeless, the friendless, the lonely. Christmas should inspire us to give generously not only to our family and friends, but to those from whom we can expect no return.

A PRAYER FOR CHRISTMAS

Father, all-powerful and ever-living God,
we do well always and everywhere to give you thanks
through Jesus Christ our Lord.
For when your only-begotten Son came among us,
a mortal man as we are,
he gave us fresh life by the new light of his immortality.

Let us pray: We ask you, O God, our Father, that your Son's birth as a human child may deliver us from the old slavery that holds us fast beneath the yoke of sin. Lord Jesus, by the example you gave us in the poverty of your birth, teach us not to become so engrossed in material things that we lose sense of the true values of life.

Spirit of love, inspire us with generosity towards people in misfortune and distress.

Preface for Christmas

Readings appropriate for the Christmas season will be found on pages 163–165.

The Easter Season

Preparation

The preparation for Easter starts with the first Sunday of Lent and continues for the following five weeks. Christians have always tried to prepare for Easter by prayer, fasting and almsdeeds.

Prayer: From time to time we need to review our habits of prayer. Lent is a good time to do so.

Towards the end of Lent we begin to think of our Lord's passion and death. For many years Christians have found that the 'Way of the Cross' is a source of prayerful thoughts on the Passion. A suggested formula is given below.

Fasting: Doing without our usual meals may not be practical now. But certainly there are plenty of ways in which we can deny ourselves (alcohol, nicotine, sweets, entertainments), and there can be no following of Christ without that. 'If anyone wants to be a follower of mine, let him renounce himself and take up his cross and follow me.' (Mark 8, 34.)

Almsdeeds: 'If a man who was rich enough in this world's goods saw that one of his brothers was in need, but closed his heart to him, how could the love of God be living in him?' (1 John, 3, 17.) There are numerous charities asking for help. The Catholic Fund for Overseas Development (Cafod) is one among many. (Cafod, 14, Howick Place, London, S.W.1.)

Readings suitable for Lent will be found on pages 165–170.

Prayers During Lent

Father all-powerful and ever-living God,
we do well always and everywhere to give you thanks
through Jesus Christ our Lord.
You bid your faithful people cleanse their hearts
and prepare with joy for the paschal feast.

More fervent in prayer,
more generous in works of charity,
more eager in celebrating the mysteries by which we are
  reborn
may we come to the fullness of grace
that belongs to the sons of God.

Let us pray: O God our Father, send us your Holy Spirit at this special time of Lent so that we may use these days well in preparing for the joyful celebration of the paschal mystery of your Son, our Lord, Jesus Christ, through whom we make this prayer to you. Amen.

THE WAY OF THE CROSS

1. Jesus is condemned to death

LEADER: Jesus, we kneel to honour you. (*All genuflect.*)

ALL: We thank you, Lord Jesus, for all you have done for us.

LEADER: Jesus was handed over to Pontius Pilate, the Roman governor. Some people did not believe him when he said that he had come from God and so they decided he must die. Because Jesus was really human like we are, he felt sad when people went against him. (*Very short pause.*)

LEADER: Let us pray.

ALL: Lord Jesus, our Saviour, we need you. Help us to love and follow you. Help us to see and serve you in everyone we meet.

This is the format of each station. The following lines give only the thoughts for each individual station.

2. Jesus carries his cross
The cross was heavy and the journey about half a mile, through narrow streets. Some people along the way were interested, but many just went on with their business. They did not know or care that their Saviour was passing by.

3. Jesus falls the first time
Jesus was weak before he started this journey because of all he had suffered already. This weakness and the weight of the cross made him fall to the ground.

4. Jesus meets his mother
Mary felt very sad when she met her Son and she wished that she could have helped him. She had looked after him when he was small but now she could do nothing for him except to let him know that she was there.

5. Simon helps Jesus
Simon didn't want to help Jesus at first. He was ashamed to be with a common criminal. We too are sometimes ashamed to do what is right because of what our friends will say. Then we have to be like Simon.

6. Veronica wipes the face of Jesus
Veronica was sorry for Jesus and wanted to help him. When we help those who suffer in any way, we are helping Jesus.

7. Jesus falls the second time
Perhaps Jesus was half way through the journey when

he fell. He hadn't got very far to go and he struggled to his feet to carry on because he knew that this was how he would save us.

8. Jesus meets the women

Jesus knew that he was soon going to die. Like all of us he didn't want to suffer and he was frightened. Even so, he thought of others. These women were sad because of him and so he spoke to them and consoled them.

9. Jesus falls the third time

Now he is near the top of calvary hill and he is exhausted even though Simon has been helping him. Perhaps he can't see properly where he is walking and he slips and falls to the ground.

10. Jesus is stripped of his clothes

Nearly all Jesus' friends had left him. His own people had turned against him. Now his clothes are taken off him in public; he loses even his dignity. No one likes to be made fun of, but Jesus himself said nothing.

11. Jesus is crucified

Cruel men had brought about his death but Jesus accepted it. If he had run away, he knew that he would not have been able to give the message his Father had asked him to bring to men. Mary didn't run away either, she stayed close to the cross so that she might be our mother.

12. Jesus dies

Jesus had said, 'The greatest proof of your love is to give your life for your friends'. He did this himself to show just how much God loves us his friends. We will always stay his friend if we try to do what he wants us to do.

13. The body of Jesus is taken down from the cross

The ordinary life of Jesus is finished. But his special life is soon to begin. By his special life he is with us all the time. He is our friend and brother and he never leaves us. He never stops loving us even though we may sometimes stop loving him.

14. The body of Jesus is put in the tomb
The tomb was made of rock. There they laid the body of Jesus. On Easter Sunday the Father raised him high and gave him the name which is above all other names so that everyone should honour Jesus as the Lord.

LEADER: May our Lord Jesus be always with you.

ALL: And also with you.

Let us pray (*pause*).

LEADER OR ALL: Dear God our Father, look kindly on your family. It was for this family of yours that your Son, our Lord Jesus suffered and died at the hands of cruel men.

May your Holy Spirit, the Spirit that filled Jesus, lead us to spend our lives as he did in the loving service of others.

We make this prayer to you through this same Jesus who lives united with you by the Spirit for ever and ever. Amen.

Celebration

'Holy Mother Church considers it her duty to celebrate the saving working of her divine Spouse by devoutly recalling it to mind on certain days throughout the course of the year. Every week, on the day which she has called "The Lord's Day", she keeps the memory of her Lord's resurrection; once in the year, by the most solemn festival of the Pasch, she

celebrates his resurrection together with his passion.'
(Vatican II Constitution on the Liturgy.)

The celebration of Easter begins on Holy Thursday when the last supper is commemorated by Mass in the evening. On Good Friday afternoon we remember our Lord's death by a special service of prayers and readings culminating in a communion service. Late at night before Easter Sunday there takes place the most solemn ceremony of the whole year: the service commemorating joyfully the passing over of Jesus to his Father. In the readings and prayers we first recall the passing over from slavery to freedom of the Hebrews, then we gratefully thank God for our own similar passing over from death to life in baptism when we were inserted into the living body of Christ – his Church.

The word 'Alleluia' is used frequently between Easter and the Pentecost. It is derived from two Hebrew words: 'hallel' meaning 'praise' and 'yah' meaning 'God'. In this season we constantly say 'Praise be to God' in grateful recognition of all he has done for us through His beloved Son, Jesus Christ.

Readings appropriate to this time will be found on pages 171–175.

PRAYERS FOR EASTERTIDE

Father, all-powerful and ever-living God,
We do well always and everywhere to give you thanks
But more especially at this time when Christ, our pasch, was sacrificed.
For he is the true lamb that has taken away the sins of the world.
By dying he overcame our death and by rising again he restored our life.

O God our Father, at Easter time we remember the great hope of eternal life which you have set before us and we feel within our hearts longings for goodness and for you. Grant that nothing may hinder the hope of eternal life from coming true, and the desire for goodness and for you from being realised.

Grant, O God,
that we may never lose the way through our self-will,
    and so end up in the far countries of the soul;
that we may never abandon the struggle,
    but that we may endure to the end,
    and so be saved;
that we may never drop out of the race,
    but that we may ever press forward
    to the goal of our high calling;
that we may never choose the cheap and passing things,
    and let go the precious things that last for ever;
that we may never take the easy way,
    and so leave the right way;
that we may never forget
    that sweat is the price of all things,
    and that without the cross, there cannot be the crown.

So keep us and strengthen us by your grace that no disobedience and no weakness and no failure may stop us from entering into the blessedness which awaits those who are faithful in all the changes and the chances of life down even to the gates of death; through Jesus Christ our Lord. Amen.*

*This prayer is taken from William Barclay's *Prayers for the Christian Year* (S.C.M. London 1964). This book and *Prayers and Epilogues* by the same author cannot be recommended too highly.

'He ascended into heaven sits at the right hand of the Father.' We do not need to think that at the ascension Jesus left us. The ascension is a symbolical gesture to show that his earthly, visible existence is at an end. It sets the seal on the accomplishment of his work.

'Sits at the right hand of the Father' again is not literal language, it is a metaphor meaning that Jesus now shares the Father's power and is able to send us the Holy Spirit, his Spirit.

The apostles prayed for the coming of the Spirit. 'When they (the disciples) reached the city (Jerusalem) they went to the upper room where they were staying. . . . All these joined in continuous prayer, together with several women, including Mary the mother of Jesus . . . (Acts 1, 13–14.)

During the nine days between ascension day and Whit Sunday (Pentecost Sunday) the prayers on pages 41 and 44 are suitable. The Latin word for nine is novem – hence the word 'novena'. Readings on pages 173–175 are appropriate.

Whit Sunday ends the paschal season.

Index

C

Canon of the Mass – *see* Eucharistic Prayers

M

O

P